The Early Religious History of France

An Introduction for Church Planters and Missionaries

Also by David R. Dunaetz

Personality and Conflict Style: Effects on Membership Duration in Voluntary Associations

THE EARLY RELIGIOUS HISTORY OF FRANCE

An Introduction for Church Planters and Missionaries

David R. Dunaetz

Martel
Press

Claremont, California

Copyright 2012 by
David R. Dunaetz
All Rights Reserved

First Published in the United States of America by
Martel Press
142 Principia Court, Claremont, California 91711

16 15 14 13 12   7 6 5 4 3 2 1

ISBN-10: 0615533132
ISBN-13: 978-0615533131

Library of Congress Control Number: 2011915670

Scripture quotations taken from the New American Standard Bible®,
Copyright © 1960, 1962, 1963, 1968, 1971, 1972, 1973,
1975, 1977, 1995 by The Lockman Foundation
Used by permission. (www.Lockman.org)

CONTENTS

Introduction 1

1. The Pre-Christian Era: Antiquity to the Second Century 5

2. Early Christianity: The Second and Third Centuries 19

3. The Beginning of Christianity as the State Religion: The Fourth Century 33

4. The Merovingian Church: The Fifth Through Seventh Centuries 55

5. The Church Under The Carolingians: The Eighth Through Tenth Centuries 91

6. The Church In The Second And Third Millenniums 115

References Cited 127

Index 131

This book is dedicated

to all the Christian workers

who have given their lives

to proclaiming the Gospel in France

Introduction

France, long known as "The Eldest Daughter of the Church," has a religious history that is both glorious and infamous, edifying and discouraging, divine and demonic. It is a story that is incredibly complex, partly because of the complexity of the individuals and the events that it contains, partly because of the sheer volume of material that documents this aspect of its history over the millennia.

So much has been published on various periods, problems, and people that it is very difficult to get an overview of the religious history of France. One can try to extract the religious aspect of French history from studying the history of France in general, or one can attempt a synthesis by reading several works treating various subjects written from different perspectives by different authors. However, there is no single, comprehensive work in English dealing with the religious history of France.

The goal of this book is to give an overview of the religious history of France up to the year 1000 for people who want to understand how God has worked in this country throughout the ages and would like to better understand the role that God would have them play as French religious history continues to unfold. Specifically, this book is for evangelicals, especially North Americans, who have come to France as missionaries (or in other roles) to help fulfill the Great Commission.

The Relationship between French History and Culture

When one takes into consideration the great diversity of cultures in the world, North Americans are culturally near to the French. However, there are significant differences in their world-views, and how well one understands these differences will greatly influence the effectiveness of his or her ministry in France. In terms of level of education, genetic make-up and economic level, there is little that separates the average North American and French person. Yet the differences are real. Sometimes they are quite subtle, sometimes they are quite blatant. Every American tourist, even after a few days in France, comes back with a strong conviction that the French really are "French."

One of the greatest differences between North Americans and the French is their attitude towards religion. North Americans generally have a positive attitude toward Christianity and the majority have a Protestant heritage. The French, however, are generally negative in their view of Christianity and most are baptized Roman Catholic. About one out of four people in North America consider themselves evangelical Christians whereas in France it is only about one in two hundred. This, of course, is the main reason why North Americans go to France as missionaries.

Why this difference? Some of the main reasons are found in the different religious histories of these two countries.

The goal of this book is to help North Americans understand the religious history of France so that they may better understand the French and thus have a more effective ministry among them. Although many North Americans cannot appreciate the influence that history has on defining a culture, because of their own cultural bias against history in general, it seems to me that no other immutable factor (climate, geography, genetics, etc.) can claim to have a greater influence on culture.

The Areas Emphasized in This Book

In writing this book, I am assuming a missions oriented audience that has had introductory courses in Western Civilization and Church history, but whose background in French history is limited. I am also assuming that the audience's primary interest in French history lies in its missiological applications. In order to maximize the missiological relevance of this book, I have tried to emphasize the following areas.

1. *Religious History which has Influenced French Culture*: I first want to emphasize the aspects of religious history which have influenced French culture in general, thus enabling missionaries to understand why the French are the way they are and to communicate the Gospel in ways that the French can understand.

2. *Key Persons, Events, and Places*: Secondly, I want to cover the key persons, events, and places in France's religious history that are a part of general French culture. Understanding these aspects of culture will help missionaries to better relate to the French by giving them culturally

relevant reference points in their discussions concerning the Gospel and its implications.

3. *Key Factors Influencing Modern Churches*: I want to underline the parts of French religious history which have influenced (in either a positive or a negative way) today's churches, especially Protestant churches, and even more specifically evangelical Protestant churches.

4. *The Elements of French History Foreign to North Americans*: Finally, I would like to try to explain clearly the elements in France's religious history which either seem very confusing or irrelevant from a North American point of view, but which are neither confusing nor irrelevant from an educated French person's point of view.

At the beginning of the twenty-first century, France is not presently a focal point of missions recruitment. There are many reasons for this, namely that the people are nominally Christian, the Bible has long been translated into French and can be ordered from any bookstore, the country lies outside of the 10-40 Window, the people are very resistant to the Gospel, many missionaries are already working here, the minority people groups have been or are in the process of being assimilated into the dominating culture, and it is very expensive to live here. Thus it is much easier to recruit missionaries for other fields.

Nevertheless, I believe that God is still calling certain people to evangelize and plant churches among this people who so strongly wish to influence the rest of the world. It is not great quantities of missionaries that France needs, but men and women who are led by God's Spirit and Word, and who are prepared to communicate the Gospel and its implications in ways that the French can understand.

1
The Pre-Christian Era: Antiquity to the Second Century

Astérix and his friend Obélix are the principal characters in France's most popular comic book series. Each book begins, "It's 50 B.C. All of Gaul is occupied by the Romans. . . . All? No! One village populated by invincible Gauls is still resisting the invaders" (Goscinny 1975). These heroes are ubiquitous witnesses to the long history of France that has not always been Christian. With their magic potion prepared by Panoramix the Druid, they are able to withstand anything that Rome might try against them.

Pre-Roman Gaul

Although there is much speculation concerning the religion of pre-historic people in France based on scant archeological artifacts and drawings such as those found in the cave of Lascaux, we can be certain of little before the Iron

Age. However, by the eighth century B.C., things become more clear (Rivière 1986:9-10).

Celtic Origins

Before the eighth century B.C., Western Europe was inhabited by numerous tribes each seeking to defend their own interests and dominate the others. Around 750 B.C., one of these tribes, the Celts (*les Celtes*) discovered how to make iron tools and weapons and soon became the dominant people. Over the next few centuries, the Celtic influence dominated culture in what is now Ireland, Great Britain, Belgium, Southern Germany, France, Switzerland, Northern Italy, as well as parts of Greece, the Balkans, and Turkey (Rey 1987:356).

To the Mediterranean cultures (including the Greeks and Romans), the Celts of the West (Transalpine) and the Center (Cisalpine) of Europe were known as the Gauls (*les Gaulois*), and those of the East (Asia Minor) were known as the Galatians (*les Galates*). The Galatians were quickly Hellenized, but the Gauls remained fiercely independent, in spite of Greek and Roman colonization, until they were defeated by Julius Cesar (*Jules César*) in 52 B.C. after many years of resistance (Rey 1987:356).

The Celtic Religion

The religion of the Gauls needs to be understood on two levels. On the day to day level, the ordinary person worshiped many nature-based divinities, especially springs (*sources*) and rock formations (*rochers*), as well as trees, forests, and mountains. Many of these gods were local in nature, others seemed to be worshiped over the whole territory, especially the goddesses of fertility and mother-earth. The offerings made to these gods included money, miniature weapons, and small statues. At the sacred springs, the waters were believed to have healing power and were used for the immersion, the aspersion, or consumption of the worshiper. The most concrete artifacts revealing the popular religion were those used in the complex Celtic funeral rites which included sacrificial cremations and commemorative banquets to remember the dead in which the dead were said to take part (De Montclos 1988:6-7).

On the more metaphysical level, the druid (*druide*) caste dominated the scene. These social and political leaders played the role of doctors, priests, and astrologers. They organized the religious ceremonies, including both animal and human sacrifices (those chosen were primarily prisoners). Youth who were chosen to become druids underwent a long period of esoteric training. The druids from all of Gaul (except from Brittany) would meet together annually for practical networking and religious ceremonies; those from Brittany would have their own traditional meetings (De Montclos 1988:6-7; Rivière 1986:10-12).

Gaul under Roman Domination

In 52 B.C., with the defeat of the famous Gallic general Vercingétorix, Rome gained control over most of Gaul. Over the next century Gaul was fully integrated in the Roman Empire, even to the point that several emperors in the first and second centuries were born in Gaul. In the places where the Gauls had built strongholds, cities began to develop in which the use of Latin grew and the Roman culture began to be adopted by the Gauls who lived there. There was much prestige attached to Roman culture because of its technology, riches, and arts, but the Gallic language and culture continued to dominate the rural areas (Rivière 1986:12-16).

The Roman Influence on the Religion of Gaul

The Romans were quite tolerant of popular religion in their conquered lands and there was no opposition to the Gallic nature gods. However, the Romans were quite hostile towards druidism because of its tendency toward independence and rebellion against Rome's authority. Human sacrifice was not tolerated in the Roman Empire. Brittany was one of the last regions of Gaul brought under Roman control and, according to Cesar, this is where one would go to do in-depth studies of druidism's teachings. Since the metaphysical ideas of druidism were not understood by the masses, the dismantlement of druidism virtually extinguished the religious institutions of Gaul. The druids had to practice their magic in secret and eventually lost their dominant role in society by becoming simple local witches (Burnand 1996:94-95).

The Evolution of the Gallic Religion

The worship of indigenous gods continued to flourish, often being syncretistically mixed with the Roman pantheon by a practice called *interprétation*, by which a Gallic god was honored under the name of a Roman god, and vice-versa. In the upper classes, the gods tended to be more Roman in nature, and in the lower classes, they tended to be more Gallic (Burnand 1996:95).

The new Gallo-Roman pantheon consisted of three broad categories of divinities. The first category were the gods of Gaul which did not correspond to Roman gods, such as gods of animals, mother-nature goddesses, and the divinities associated with specific geological formations (rivers, springs, mountains, etc.). Although these gods were indigenous to the

Gauls, our knowledge of them comes from the fact that the Gauls eventually started to use Latin inscriptions and Roman style iconography to depict and honor them (Burnand 1996:95-96).

The second category consisted of Gallo-Roman gods assimilated by *interprétation*. Mercury was the god most commonly honored, sometimes in Gallic dress, other times in more classic forms. Mars, Apollo, Jupiter, Minerva, Vulcan and Hercules were all worshiped, in more or less Gallic forms (Burnand 1996:96-100).

The third category consists of oriental gods introduced by traders and soldiers which were never really assimilated with indigenous deities. These include Syrian Baals, the Phrygian Cybele, and Iranian Mithra. The diffusion of their worship was more limited than the Roman and Greek pantheon. These cults appear to have been adopted by those who sought personal contact with the divine and the hope of life after death. They undoubtedly helped pave the way for Christianity (Burnand 1996:100-101).

The evolution of religious practices during this period was influenced by the new art forms and technologies introduced by the Romans. For the first time, statues and monuments were erected; their goal was to thank or petition a deity. The altars used for sacrifices and oblations (the principal religious ceremonies) became more ornate. Hundreds of *ex voto* (signs of thanksgiving for answered prayer) have been found at springs in the form of the body part which had been healed (Burnand 1996:101-102).

Missiological Applications

Astérix and Obélix are not the only remnants of pre-Roman Gaul found in France today. The Celtic influence can be seen in several practices which seem bizarre, at best, and demonic, at worst, to North American evangelicals. At first glance, the missionary might be tempted to reject all that came from this early period of pre-Christian paganism. Surely, there is much to reject, but there are also important lessons to be learned.

Traditional Healing Methods

Like many religions, the Gallic religion held that healing was available to those who were properly informed. In modern France, many springs considered sacred by the Gauls are still considered today to have healing properties. Drinking from a specific spring is supposed to heal certain ailments or organs. This belief is so strong that stays of several days are partially paid for by the national health insurance program (*la sécurité sociale*) for the springs that have no direct connection with Roman Catholicism.

From a scientific point of view, it is easy to say that these beliefs are simply superstitions since double-blind tests show no specific healing powers in the waters. But since people swear by the results of these cures, it appears that the effects of these springs are essentially psychosomatic. One takes a few days vacation, goes to the mountains and does little besides standing around drinking a few glasses of water and relaxing. That would do many of us some good. Yet if a psychological dependence is formed, this dependence can be dangerous for both Christians and non-Christians. Belief in any superstition, even if the results are positive, blinds one to the truth and makes him a slave of his or her errors. Jesus said,

"The truth will make you free" (John 8:32). Since I believe that the scientific method is a legitimate way of approaching truth, I believe that a missionary should do what he or she can to correct superstitious beliefs in those who want to go beyond them so that they might more completely put their faith in Christ.

However, there are both Christians and non-Christians who reject a scientific point of view. What I would call a "superstition," they might describe as another facet of God's healing power that is beyond my comprehension. They might say that they themselves understand how it works, but that the large pharmaceutical companies are too busy promoting their own research and products to invest in the research necessary to demonstrate scientifically how these more effective treatments actually work. Or they might give some other reason why science has not been able to prove the efficacy of these alternative medicines.

A missionary who comes with a scientific point of view will find it very difficult and frustrating to argue against this sort of anti-scientific bias. But convincing people that a scientific world view is correct is not our top priority. We come to France as promoters of the Gospel, not the scientific method. It is unlikely that any of the apostles had a very scientific world view, but they effectively evangelized their world. We, too, need to focus on communicating the Gospel and helping people put their faith in Christ, whether or not they see a need to give up their springs or other sorts of "alternative medicines."

At the same time, the desire to be healed from sickness is a legitimate desire. We need to respond to this need, not with healing techniques that might be a Christianized form of alternative medicine, but with sincere prayer where both the sick and the healthy humbly come before God, seeking his healing power and infinite goodness and willingly accepting what he sees as best in the situation.

Respect for Nature

On the more positive side, the average French person, like his or her Celtic ancestors, has a very high regard for forests, rock formations (the *rochers de Fontainebleau* are especially appreciated in the Paris area), and mountains (such as the Alps, Mont St. Michel which is the site of an important abbey, and the Puy de Dôme with the ruins of a major Roman temple to Mercury). This is positive because the power of God is seen in his creation (Rom. 1:20) and is a natural revelation of his nature. The argument from nature is perhaps the most powerful argument for the existence of God, and since approximately half the population is atheist, it is an argument that is very useful in evangelism.

However, there are some Christians who would say that since these sites have been long associated with non-Christian religions, the territorial spirits or other demonic forces are especially strong there. This seems to me to be going beyond what Scripture teaches and enters into the realm of speculation (I Tim. 1:4, Tit. 3:9). Nevertheless, it is true to say that worship of vacations (*le culte des vacances),* vacations which often take place at sites that were holy to the Gauls, certainly replaces the worship of the true God in the lives of many French people.

Anti-Biblical Religious Practices

Other Gallic religious rites are still practiced in one form or another and are clearly unacceptable from a biblical point of view. Missionaries will want to adapt their teaching so that their churches avoid any sort of syncretism.

The prayers for and communication with the dead which originated with the Celtic burial practices and later associated with All Saints Day (*le Toussaint*) have long been rejected by Protestants (Lev. 20:27, Heb. 9:27), but are practiced regularly in the Catholic church. Although All Saints Day is held up as a Christian holiday, neo-paganism and globalization have also introduced American Halloween to this holiday, making it even less Christian than before.

Two other remaining elements of druidism are witchcraft and astrology. Although these practices have undoubtedly evolved over the years due to exterior influences such as the magical practices of the gypsies (*les tziganes*), the Babylonian concept of astrology, the omni-present African witch doctors (*marabouts*) in the Paris area, and fads (e.g. New Age practices), modern day witchcraft in France (and in much of the occidental world) is essentially based on esoteric practices that originated with the druids. Probably all non-Christian bookstores in France have a larger section on esoterica than on Christianity. The missionary must teach not only that these practices must be avoided, but he or she must also denounce them for what they actually are, the works of Satan (Deu. 18:9-13, Eph. 5:11).

The Conflict between Civil and Religious Authorities

Under Roman domination, we see, for the first time, a conflict between the secular (Roman) and religious authority (the druids). This is a common theme in French history, and a situation which occurs regularly in church planting efforts today. The French are not afraid of stating their opinions and having conflicts ("French" is a doublet of "frank," which means to freely speak one's mind), so the risk of a conflict with a local authority (usually the mayor, *le maire*) is very likely.

On an institutional level, Rome was stronger than druidism, and was thus able to transform it into an acceptable form. Today, the institutional power of the French state is infinitely stronger than that of evangelical churches. Any activities that disturb the authorities (national or local) can be repressed through legislation, taxation or administrative red tape. This means that a missionary needs to work with the local authorities, doing what he or she can to assure them that what he or she is doing is good, or at least acceptable, in their sight. Fortunately, most authorities are fairly reasonable and tolerant and human rights are emphasized by the national press and authorities.

However, there is a significant fear of cults. The government has occasionally classified some evangelical groups as cults, thus considering them dangerous and worthy of repression. Certainly the missionary does not want to compromise any biblical fundamentals, but he or she would be wise to nurture his or her relationship with local authorities and do all that is possible so that the young church would be viewed favorably.

A healthy relationship with authorities is crucial. It is especially useful when asking for the use of city buildings for various activities, when an appropriate building permit is needed, or when one would like to obtain positive coverage in the local press.

Cultural Prestige

Another missiological application comes from observing that the Roman religion was easily incorporated into the Gallic religion partly because of the prestige associated with Roman culture. Today, North American missionaries bring with them both the prestige and the infamy of American culture, a culture that leaves no French person unmoved.

Whereas our cultural background, which is heard every time most of us open our mouths, may open doors to explain why we are here, we must be careful that we ultimately draw people to the message of Christ and not simply to positive aspects of American culture that North American missionaries tend to specialize in (friendliness, humor, compassion, pragmatics, etc.) which would be a simple formula for syncretism.

At the same time, missionaries need to be sensitive to Gallic independence, an attitude that is still strong. Astérix, although a cartoon character, is a national hero. He is short, old, complaining and not especially very nice. But he fights against the Romans. Vercingétorix, the historical figure who served as a rough model for Astérix, is a hero because he was the last to fall to Roman domination.

Even if a missionary is very sensitive to French culture, seeking only to import ideas based on the Gospel, it is likely that he or she will be accused of importing Americanization as well, whether it is true or not. The French are extremely aware of their cultural identity. Perhaps the best approach is to adopt a position of Gallic independence as well. The missionary can appeal to those in leadership to find French ways of doing things. When he or she sees negative aspects of American culture, he can be the first to criticize them. When he or she notices that someone is bothered by his or her accent, he or she can be the first to make a joke about it. When he or she sees someone adopting something neutral or even seemingly positive coming from America (such as various electronic gadgets or fast-food), he or she can be the first to question it. These attitudes can help the missionary gain respect and help those he or she works with come to or grow in Christ without losing their French identity.

Bridges to the Gospel

Several of the Gallic religious concepts which have survived over the centuries form bridges that make understanding Biblical ideas easier, though they do not especially do anything to convince the person of his or her need to respond to the Gospel. The idea of sacrifice, giving something to a divinity to appease his or her anger or to assure his or her goodwill, has existed throughout the centuries. In all Catholic churches there is still an altar, and the mass (the sacrifice) is the focal point of normal religious ceremonies. Thus the idea of one's need for a sacrifice is not especially foreign to a French person. The stumbling block comes from the fact that we believe that Christ's sacrifice was sufficient once and for all and that one needs to respond by putting his or her faith in God.

A second aspect of Gallic religion that plays a part in biblical Christianity is thanksgiving. In pre-Christian Gaul, this was manifested by the construction of temples and monuments dedicated to the deities. In the Christian period, it was manifested by the construction of churches and cathedrals in order to thank the Saints. *Ex voto* (signs of thanksgiving) have existed for two thousand years in France; small marble plaques (especially from the nineteenth and early twentieth centuries) cover many a wall in Catholic churches.

This background enables evangelical Christians to put a healthy emphasis on thanksgiving and worship in the church. It is not a difficult idea to introduce to non-Christians or new Christians. Usually the worship and thanksgiving time in a Sunday morning service is longer than the sermon in French evangelical churches, which is often not the case in North America.

An idea perhaps worthy of consideration which I have not yet seen put into practice is to use the importance of thanksgiving to help finance building projects. Almost all evangelical churches in France eventually find it appropriate to buy or construct their own meeting place in order to have a centralized location for their activities and to have a permanent, visible witness in their community. It seems that an idea that is worthy of further development and experimentation is that of "*ex voto* financing" of building projects. Since World War II, most evangelical churches have constructed buildings either with foreign funds or by borrowing, often resulting in the church being unable to support a pastor either because it never really learned to give (having been dependent on foreign funds) or because of the need to pay its debt. This is an important hindrance to church growth.

When North American missionaries start a fund raising campaign for a building in France, their natural tendency is to use the American logic of "Building for the Future" to try to motivate people, so that with the new building, they may better serve the Lord in the future. But French evangelicals have a tendency to think less about the future than Americans do. They tend to think that God or the State (or some combination of the two) will take care of the future, an idea that is not completely without biblical support (Mat. 6:33). Perhaps it would be more effective and culturally relevant to ask the believers to give as a sign of thanksgiving for what the Lord has already done in their life.

The Hidden Remnants of Druidism

Another missiological application concerns the remnants of druid magic and witchcraft. Ever since the Roman times, authorities have looked with disfavor upon sorcery, perhaps fearing the loss of authority, perhaps by desire to purge society of superstitions. The result is that most all sorcery is practiced in private and not discussed openly, at least not among the ethnically French. This means that a missionary must develop a solid, trusting relationship before he or she might find out about this aspect of a person's background. Many French people have had experiences with the occult and it is a theme that needs to be dealt with regularly in a young church from a Biblical point of view, even though it remains hidden in our normal everyday interactions with people.

It is interesting to note that Brittany is one of the regions of France that is the most resistant to the Gospel, as well as the region most known for its witchcraft and fervent Catholicism. Although it is impossible to say with certainty that these facts are related, two thousand years ago Julius Cesar also remarked that these people were different from the others in Gaul because druidism was so deeply rooted there (Burnand 1996:94).

Apart from natural revelation, it is likely the Gauls were without witness to the one true and living God. The religion of druidism, later diluted and mixed with the Roman pantheon, could not lead to a knowledge of the Truth. Yet, at the same time across the Mediterranean Sea, Jesus Christ had come to earth, lived as a man, was crucified, and rose from the dead. News of the Son of God and his teaching would soon arrive in Gaul, bringing about changes far greater than what the Romans had wrought.

2
Early Christianity: The Second and Third Centuries

Christianity seems to have spread more slowly in Gaul than in the rest of the Roman Empire. We do not know if this was because the Gauls were more resistant to the Gospel, because the persecution was greater there, because there was less missionary activity in the region, or simply because most of the traces of early Christianity in Gaul have been lost. But in any case, the message of the Gospel eventually arrived, and it immediately started to transform lives (De Montclos 1988:8-9).

The First Christians

There are no historical records indicating how the Gospel arrived in Gaul, who the first Christians were, or where the first churches were started. However, by the end of the second century, we see that churches were firmly implanted in several cities (Burnand 1996:102).

The Second Century Church in Lyons and Vienne

The earliest record we have of Christianity in Gaul is the letter from the Christians of Lyons (*Lyon*) and Vienne, probably under the leadership of Irenaeus (*Irénée*), the second pastor (traditionally called the bishop) of Lyons, that was written to churches in Asia to describe the persecution the church in the Rhone Valley had undergone in 177. The parts of this letter that we have available to us are found in the works of Eusebius (324:139-150).

These churches, Lyons and Vienne, are the first known churches west of Rome. Pothinus, the first pastor of these churches, and Irenaeus were both most likely from Asia (based on Irenaeus' descriptions of their youth), perhaps coming to Gaul for commerce or for missionary work. The churches seem to be mixed both ethnically and economically. Irenaeus mentions that he carried out his ministry in both the Gallic language of the common person and in Latin, the language of the culturally elite. One of the church members who was among the first martyrs, Vettius Epagathus, came from a well to do senatorial family. Others were rich enough to have servants. But also, there were servants in the congregation, such as Blandina (*Blandine*), the most famous of the martyrs of Lyons (Burnand 1996:102).

Roman authorities in the Rhone Valley began persecuting the Christians in the region because they were considered irreligious and atheists, refusing to worship the Roman gods. The persecution began as a simple prohibition to frequent public places. Then hatred of the Christians grew until some were attacked by mobs. Some were dragged into courts and jailed. The governor of the district hated the

Christians and ordered that all of the most active members of the two churches be arrested, as well as their servants. Some of these non-believing servants, wanting to disassociate themselves from the Christians began accusing them of cannibalism and incest. This resulted in those imprisoned being tortured. Several were also fed to wild beasts or burned in the amphitheater, but most were left to die in the filthy prisons (De Montclos 1988:9).

I believe it is worth citing several passages of the letter written by these churches, describing what they saw one of their members go through:

> The whole fury of crowd, governor, and soldiers fell with crushing force . . . on Blandina, through whom Christ proved that things which men regard as mean, unlovely, and contemptible are by God deemed worthy of great glory, because of her love for Him shown in power and not vaunted in appearance. When we were all afraid, . . . lest she should be unable even to make a bold confession of Christ because of bodily weakness, Blandina was filled with such power that those who took it in turns to subject her to every kind of torture from morning to night were exhausted by their efforts and confessed themselves beaten--they could think of nothing else to do to her. They were amazed that she was still breathing, for her whole body was mangled and her wounds gaped; they declared that torment of any one kind was enough to part soul and body, let alone a succession of torments of such extreme severity. But the blessed woman, wrestling magnificently, grew in strength as she proclaimed her faith, and found refreshment, rest, and insensibility to her sufferings in uttering the words: 'I am a Christian: we do nothing to be ashamed of.' . . .

[On another day] Blandina was hung on a post and exposed as food for the wild beasts let loose in the arena. She looked as if she was hanging in the form of a cross, and through her ardent prayers she stimulated great enthusiasm in [the others] undergoing their ordeal. . . . As none of the beasts had yet touched her, she was taken down from the post and returned to the jail, to be kept for a second ordeal, that by victory in further contests she might make irrevocable the sentence passed on the crooked Serpent, and spur on her brother Christians--a small, weak, despised woman who had put on Christ, the great invincible champion. . . .

To crown all this, on the last day of the sports, Blandina was again brought in, and with her Ponticus, a lad of about fifteen. Day after day they had been taken in to watch the rest being punished, and attempts were made to make them swear by the heathen idols. When they stood firm and treated these efforts with contempt, the mob was infuriated with them, so that the boy's tender age called forth no pity and the woman no respect. They subjected them to every horror and inflicted every punishment in turn, attempting again and again to make them swear, but to no purpose. Ponticus was encouraged by his sister in Christ, so that the heathen saw that she was urging him on and stiffening his resistance, and he bravely endured every punishment till he gave back his spirit to God. Last of all, like a noble mother who had encouraged her children and sent them before her in triumph to the King, blessed Blandina herself passed through all the ordeals of her children and hastened to rejoin them, rejoicing and exulting at her departure as if invited to a wedding supper, not thrown to the beasts. After the whips, after the beasts, after the griddle [red hot copper plates pressed against the most sensitive parts of the body], she was finally dropped into a basket and thrown to a bull. Time after time the animal tossed her, but she was indifferent now to all that happened to her, because of her hope and sure hold on all that her faith meant, and of her communing with Christ. Then she, too, was sacrificed, while the heathen themselves admitted that never yet had they known a woman suffer so much or so long (Eusebius 324:141-147).

And so begins the history of the church in Gaul!

The persecution of 177 was a horrible ordeal for the churches. All the leaders including Pothinus the pastor were put to death. Only the Christians who had not been vocal in their faith were left. Throughout the second and third centuries, the Christians were persecuted for atheism (the refusal to sacrifice to the gods) or *lèse-majesté* (attacking the majesty of the emperor). Often the Christian could be liberated of the charges if he or she abjured by sacrificing to the idols, swearing by the emperor, sacrificing to him, or by denying Christ. Some professing Christians did deny the faith. Observing them do this was an ordeal perhaps more painful than the physical ones the faithful suffered (Rivière 1986:16).

This same letter written by the churches in Lyons and Vienne also revealed two other problems with which the early Christians had to deal. The first concerned the veneration of martyrs (witnesses). The author of the letter described that when those who managed to survive torture and prison returned to their church, those who had not gone through the ordeals wanted to grant upon them the title of martyr. However, they refused this title and wanted all the glory to go to Christ, and to the memory of those who earned their martyrdom through death (Eusebius 324:148). Although these Christians were probably pure in their motives in wanting to honor those who had been faithful to Christ amidst the persecution, we unfortunately see the first seedlings of an unhealthy veneration of saints.

The other noteworthy problem addressed in this letter concerned asceticism. One man, Alcibiades, decided to partake of bread and water only, both in and out of prison. To another Christian in the church it was somehow revealed (through a prophecy or by some other means permitting this conclusion) that what Alcibiades was doing was not right. Alcibiades accepted this and began to eat normally, giving thanks to God for all things (Eusebius 324:149-150).

After Pothinus, Irenaeus became the principal pastor in the Rhone Valley. It is possible that he had not been very involved in the church up to this point since he was not imprisoned during the persecution of 177. But he soon became the greatest Christian writer of the second century as Eusebius would call him (324:127). His most famous work is *Against Heresies* (Contre les hérésies), written in Greek for a broad audience. He desired to bring heretics back to the faith and to prevent Christians from following their errors. He used Scripture as authority, which he saw directly linked to the Apostles. However he did not see the need to differentiate between Scripture and tradition; Scripture was authoritative because it recorded apostolic tradition and the tradition handed down in the church was authoritative because it faithfully reflected the Gospel.

Irenaeus felt that the church of Rome especially represented an unbroken chain of faithfulness to the apostolic tradition, but he did not go as far as to give the church in Rome the preeminence over other churches. It is likely that one factor for his high regard for the church in Rome is based on a common Latin heritage, but he did not consider its bishop to be infallible. For example, he felt free to differ with Victor, the first bishop of Rome who spoke Latin (the language of the learned, rather than Greek), who had threatened to excommunicate other bishops who disagreed with him concerning the importance given to the date of Easter (Douglas 1978:516-17).

Irenaeus also argued for the unity and inspiration of both the Old and New Testaments and the full divinity and humanity of Christ, although he accepted the authority of such works as *The Shepherd of Hermas* and believed that the Septuagint was the inspired version of the Old Testament (Eusebius 324:155-156).

The Spread of Christianity to Other Cities

In the third century, we know that the Gospel spread to other cities in Gaul. By the end of the third century, the number of cities with churches grew to about two dozen. In 249, in the midst of persecutions throughout the Empire, seven ordained pastors/bishops were sent (most likely from Rome) to evangelize seven cities in Gaul: Tours, Arles, Narbonne, Toulouse, Paris, Clermont-Ferrand, and Limoges. Saturnius (*Saturnin*) who went to Toulouse and Dionysius (*St. Denis*) who went to Paris both became martyrs and are the best known of these missionaries (Gregory of Tours 59:86-87).

Legend has made *St. Denis* one of the great figures of French religious history. After being beheaded at Montmartre in Paris, he supposedly walked several miles north with his head in his hands until he expired where the town of St. Denis now stands. A first church was built on the site of his tomb in 475 and almost all of the kings of France, beginning with Dagobert in the seventh century, were buried there. In the twelfth century, an immense cathedral in a new style was built at this site which became the prototype for all Gothic architecture. To purify France of its superstitions, during the decade following the Revolution, the city of St. Denis was renamed "Franciade" because of its emotional importance. Even in modern history, this city was chosen to be the site of the National Stadium, *Stade de France*, where the World Cup (*Coupe du monde*) was played in 1998.

St. Denis and the rest of these seven missionaries started churches in each of the cities to which they were sent and spent the rest of their lives working there. Their disciples went on to evangelize other cities, about which we have enough information to understand a little of their early church planting strategy. For example, Ursinus (*Ursin*), a disciple of one of the original seven, went to Bourges to start a church. During his early ministry, only a few people became believers, mainly from among the poor. Ursinus appointed leaders and, according to Gregory of Tours (591:87), he taught them specifically three things: How to sing praise songs, how to structure church buildings, and how to perform ceremonies. Since the new Christians were poor, they were not able to construct a church, but they were able to save enough money to buy a house to meet in. Nevertheless, none of the homeowners in the city would sell to them since none of them wanted to go against the Roman religion. Finally, they found one property owner who felt it would be an honor for his house to be used for a church. He sold it to them for a symbolic sum (one percent of what they had offered) and later became a Christian. This new location facilitated their meetings and helped the church to grow (Gregory of Tours 591:87-88).

The great persecution of the Emperor Diocletian in the first decade of the 4th century was applied only mildly and without violence in France, being limited to the destruction of Christian books and meeting places. The reason for this attenuated persecution was perhaps because the governor of Gaul, Constance Chlore, was somewhat sympathetic towards the Christians, since one of his concubines, Hélène, was a believer. Constance Chlore later became emperor, and their son would soon become Constantine the Great (Latourette 1975:90-91).

Missiological Applications

This period of French church history is rich in missiological applications. Like now, France was clearly a mission field and the few churches that existed were young and dynamic.

Ethnic Diversity

Given the diversity of linguistic origins of the names of the early French martyrs, the early church in France seems to have been quite ethnically diverse. Comparing this with the French evangelical churches of today, a missionary may find comfort in knowing that cultural diversity is not new to French churches. The difficulties involved in managing a multi-cultural group are numerous, but not insurmountable. It is encouraging to note that the main problems that Irenaeus recorded dealt with false doctrines and persecution, not with conflicts between cultures (e.g. Acts 6:1-6). Since today's missionaries, especially in the Paris region tend to start ethnically diverse churches, they must continually deal with cultural differences and misunderstandings, but following the example set by Irenaeus, they must remember that faithfulness to Christ and His Word are much more fundamental to the life of the church. If a church is faithfully putting into practice what Jesus taught, the problems arising from cultural diversity will be less severe.

In fact, it might be possible to profit from the ethnic diversity of these young churches. At the beginning of the twenty-first century, multiculturalism and tolerance is certainly in style in France. Although the typical French person might not actively seek out situations where these values are demonstrated, these qualities are upheld as virtually divine principles by politicians and the media. Two great fears felt to some degree or another by the majority of the French concern the Neo-Nazi far right political parties *(l'extrême droite)* and violence in the inner city *(les banlieues,* which geographically means "the suburbs," but has the same socio-cultural sense as a North American "inner city.") The popular solution to these two social woes is more tolerance, less racism, and greater ethnic diversity. Unfortunately however, the vast majority of French do not feel very at ease in a social situation with poor immigrants with vastly different educational backgrounds. Nevertheless, the multi-ethnic nature of the evangelical churches can be an asset when dealing with idealistic individuals and when negotiating with politicians concerning building permits or other actions which require official approval.

Scriptural Authority

Irenaeus did not clearly distinguish between the authority of Scripture and of tradition, undoubtedly because he did not see a difference. This temptation still exists for today's church planting missionaries, in either of two forms. First of all, they might want to incorporate American traditions into the church falsely believing them to be Biblically founded or so excellent that they must be God's will, regardless of their cultural relevance (e.g. Sunday School before church, 11:00 A.M. Sunday services, worship teams for leading singing, twenty-five minute sermons). Secondly, the traditions that the missionaries themselves introduce (which might very well be culturally relevant to the French and appropriate at the beginning of a young church's history) risk becoming institutionalized and irreplaceable even when the church matures and their utility ceases to be optimal (e.g. the presence of the pastor at all meetings or the use of photocopied song sheets). The solution to this problem is to have a clear understanding and commitment to the essentials of the Gospel, a flexible spirit when it comes to designing the actual activities of the church (I Cor. 9:19-27), and teaching the church that methods can and need to change, but that the message of the Gospel never changes. This, of course, is easier said than done, given our psychological weaknesses which tend to assimilate whatever we are currently doing to that which we believe is God's unchangeable will.

Understanding the Glory of Rome

It is perhaps difficult for the North American missionary to appreciate the prestige associated with Rome which was important to the early Gallic church, and which to this day has continued to be an important value for many people in France. Perhaps a legitimate modern-day comparison is with the Founding Fathers of America. Quite often American evangelical Christians refer to the values of George Washington, Thomas Jefferson, Benjamin Franklin, Thomas Paine, Alexander Hamilton and others to describe how things should be, regardless of the fact that many of these men held beliefs and values that were blatantly non-Christian and anti-Biblical. In the same way, many French still consider the Roman church to be surrounded by a certain aura, not because of what the church teaches, but because of the majesty of its ancient culture and empire, as well as the accumulated glory of nearly two thousand years of primacy among the "Universal Church." So, it is well worth the effort of a missionary to try to speak of Rome and the Pope with respect, and to be on good terms with the local priest if he or she wishes to gain credibility even among nominal Catholics.

The Witness of the Martyrs

Another practical application from this period of church history in France comes from the example of the early martyrs. Although the number of French killed for their faith was limited in comparison to other parts of the Empire, Pothinus, Sanctus, Blandina, Saturnius, and Dionysius were all real Christians who were willing to die for Jesus Christ. The difficulties that a North American missionary will face will be significant, and the opposition that he or she will run into will be painful, but that which we are asked to give to the Lord is pittance in comparison to the sacrifices that these early Christians made. This fact should be an encouragement to us during the more trying times which tend to occur fairly often in church planting in France.

An Alternative Church Planting Model

The seven missionaries sent to Gaul in the third century present a model of church planting radically different from the one used by the majority of modern North American missionaries. Once these apostles arrived in a city, they settled there and spent the rest of their lives there. It is quite likely that they lived in near poverty at the beginning of their ministry and once the church was started, they received their support from the local congregation. They did not move on and start new churches, but they sent those they mentored to evangelize other cities. Although their results were comparable to modern day church planting statistics for a corresponding number of missionaries (a maximum of two dozen churches planted in fifty years by seven missionaries), they did produce churches which were solid, stable, and self-reproducing. North American missionaries tend to spend much shorter times in churches (five to fifteen years) but it cannot be said that this necessarily produces churches that are truly viable, even though it looks good to our constituency to say that we have moved on from one church to work on starting another.

In spite of its inherent inefficiency (each missionary would only be able to offer his life to one church, and, given our sinful nature, it might not be offered for the right reasons), it seems to me that lifetime pastoral leadership might have its advantages, such as total integration into the community, a symbiotic dependence between the missionary and the congregation, a truly incarnate ministry, leadership training focused on church planting. Perhaps missionaries (and missions) should be open to God's leading in this direction, even if it might eventually lead to minimal economic and relational ties with North America.

3
The Beginning of Christianity as the State Religion: The Fourth Century

Perhaps during no other century did so many changes occur within French Christianity. Because these transformations occurred so long ago, they do not especially seem relevant today. But if we are to effectively present the Gospel today, it will be immensely beneficial to understand this crucial century which gave Roman Christianity a place in Gallic culture which has not greatly changed up to our present time.

The Cultural Transformation of the Fourth Century

In the fourth century, two imperial decisions had an immense impact on the Gallic church. They transformed the

Empire from a world where Christianity was illegal to a world where Roman Christianity was the state religion (DeMontclos 1988:10).

The Edict of Milan

In 313 the co-Emperors Constantine (*Constantin,* Caesar of the Gauls, and Emperor of the West) and Licinius (Emperor of the East) met in Milan and took actions which gave legal recognition to Christianity and to assure the protection of Christians. No longer was it forbidden to follow Christ (Burnand 1996:103).

The traditional story of Constantine's conversion is that, during a struggle for imperial power in the West in the spring of 312, Constantine had a vision of a cross before a battle accompanied by the order, "In this sign, conquer." In October of that year, Constantine had the victory, and concluded that his success was due to the superiority of Christianity over polytheism (Latourette 1975:91-92).

Although he kept his pagan title *pontifex maximus* (chief priest of the traditional pagan religion) and was baptized only shortly before his death, Constantine favored Christianity and made a number of decisions that pleased Christians. He gave Christian pastors the same tax exemption as pagan ministers; he banned executions by crucifixion; civil workers were given Sunday as a holiday; he allowed public funds to be used to make church buildings. As early as 314, Constantine organized a Council at Arles in the South of France, calling for the Gallic bishops to mediate in the Donatist controversy ravaging the North African church (Latourette 1975:92-93).

Constantine's children were brought up as Christians and three of his sons reigned as emperor, all of them favoring Christianity. Then, in 361, one of Constantine's nephews, Julian the Apostate, became emperor and abolished the privileges that Christians had. He reestablished paganism and allowed local persecutions to break out against Christians. However, he was only emperor for two years, and those following him were more favorable to Christianity (Latourette 1975:94).

The Christianization of the Masses

The second major imperial decree occurred in 380 when Theodosius (*Théodose*) banned the pagan polytheistic religions, declaring that all people should follow the divine religion that Peter had preached to the Romans. He thus united Christianity with the State, making the emperor the chief defender of the church (Burnand 1996:103).

What are the reasons for this major cultural transformation? Although it is impossible to know Constantine's and Theodosius' exact motives, several factors can be noted. The use of Roman and Greek academic methods by Clement and Origen (from the Alexandrian school of thought) had lifted the separation between Classic culture and Christianity. Christians had also begun to integrate into Roman life at all levels, and in some of the most Christianized areas of the Empire, Christianity was already becoming the culture of the masses. From a practical point of view, the emperors were losing hold of their power due to the barbarian invasions. So, uniting the church and state gave them greater legitimacy (De Montclos 1988:10).

Since all other forms of religious expression were prohibited, Gaul was completely opened to Christianization. The results of this transformation are numerous. First of all, the sense of being Gallic and Christian increased in popular thought, as the thought of being Roman diminished. No longer was the Roman Empire held together by a religion that had evolved into emperor worship. Rather, one's cultural identity was found in Christianity (De Montclos 1988:10).

Secondly, for the first time, the landed aristocracy and high dignitaries entered into the church in large numbers. From these families came more and more new bishops, especially as the social importance of the urban middle class (where previous bishops came from) declined due to the general cultural decay of the last centuries of the Roman Empire. In this way control of the bishoprics (*évêchés*) began to be passed from the hands of the community of believers to those of important and powerful families (De Montclos 1988:10).

Christianity, in one form or another, spread over all of urbanized Gaul. By the end of the fourth century, virtually all of the 114 Roman cities (*les cités*) had a bishop. The bishoprics and the *cités* covered the same geographic areas so that the demarcations separating the responsibilities between religious and civil administrations became less and less clear. Because the bishops now possessed greater civil powers (salaries of church workers, administration of funds for the poor, close association with the emperor), the authority and prestige of bishops increased, even to the point of veneration (De Montclos 1988:11).

Since the only religious expression that was now legal was Christianity, the church had to accept everyone who was interested regardless of their religious convictions or lack thereof. Previously, the church was composed of individuals who consciously chose to be followers of Christ, often at great personal expense. But now Christianity had become the religion of the masses, regardless of a person's understanding of the Gospel. Defining who was a Christian was no longer done on the basis of a personal confession of faith, but rather on an early form of political correctness (De Montclos 1988:11).

Martin and Early Monasticism

With the influx of the masses and the loss of the purifying effects of persecution, the churches grew both in numbers and in worldliness. One of the responses to this worldliness was the rise of monasticism (*monachisme*). Since being a Christian no longer necessarily meant being different than the unconverted, many of those who were truly committed to Jesus Christ sought new ways to manifest their dedication to him. In the Eastern Empire of the fourth century, this was manifested by both anchoritic (solitary) and cenobitic (communal) monasticism. However, in Gaul, the monastic ideal was mostly limited to the latter, introduced to France by Martin of Tours (De Montclos 1988:11).

It is hard to underestimate the importance of Martin in French church history. Whereas the martyrs of Lyons and Vienne and the seven missionaries sent to evangelize Gaul manifested their commitment to Christ in ways that conservative evangelical Protestants can easily understand, Martin introduced an alternate lifestyle (monasticism) that would be adopted and encouraged by the church for all who wanted to manifest a true commitment to Christ, but which is very different from today's evangelical Protestantism. In addition, he was the first to carry out a multi-regional evangelization program in France. Because of his biography, *The Life of Martin* written by his friend and disciple Sulpicius Severus (*Sulpice Sévère*), his renown for miracle working advanced with the centuries (Burnand 1996:105).

Martin, born in modern Hungary, was a soldier with the Roman army who at one point shared his cloak with a poor beggar at Amiens (in the north of France). Soon afterwards, he had a vision of Christ and this resulted in his conversion. He was baptized and, after being discharged from the army, worked alongside the bishop Hillary of Poitiers (*Hillaire de Poitiers*). In 361, he founded the first French monastery, at Ligué near Poitiers, and in 371 he was chosen to be the bishop of Tours, though he continued to live a simple life and refused to sit on the bishop's throne. He was active in the formation of other monasteries in France and he seriously undertook the evangelization of the rural areas of France (Douglas 1978:638).

Martin was in some ways a counter-cultural hero and fourth century version of Vercingétorix. Many in the established church did not like him. "A person with such a scruffy appearance, dirty clothes and unkempt hair was unworthy of the episcopate" (Severus c. 395:143). In addition to not fitting the cultural expectation of what a religious leader was to be like, he was also one of the few in the church not willing to compromise with the civil authorities. As Severus said, "Our age has become so depraved and corrupted that it is almost exceptional for a priest to have the strength not to yield to flattery of the emperor" (c. 395:152).

Since Martin was in some sense the father of the church in Gaul (at least in this new cultural context), his tomb became an important pilgrimage center because of the prestige of his name and relics. In the first half of the 2nd millennium, when family names became permanent, *Martin* was the one chosen the most often. Today, it is the cultural equivalent of "Smith" and twice as many people share this family name as those who have the second most common, *Bernard* (Frémy and Frémy 1998:1328).

Martin had no "Rule" (the functional equivalent of a church constitution, doctrinal statement, and by-laws in modern evangelical North American churches) for the monasteries he founded. His goal for the monks and nuns was simply that they live a communal life in order to better serve Christ, being separated from the world and its corrupting influences. "All of his conversation with us was concerned with the need to leave behind the seductions of this world and our secular burdens so that, free and untrammelled, we might follow the Lord Jesus" (Severus c. 395:157).

The popular image of monks living in great stone monasteries is only applicable to those of the eleventh century and onwards. Very few buildings were made of stone in France between the fourth and the tenth centuries, and the very idea of such a lifestyle would be quite foreign to Martin and his followers.

> Martin lived in a small cell made of wood and a number of the brothers lived in a similar manner, but most of them had made shelters for themselves by hollowing out the rock of the mountain which overlooked the place. There were about eighty disciples who had chosen to lead a life in accordance with their blessed master's example. No one there possessed anything of his own, everything was shared. They were not allowed to buy or sell anything (as is the practice with most monks). No craft was practiced there, apart from the scribes; the young were set to this task while the older ones spent their time in prayer. It was rare for anyone to leave his own cell except when they gathered at the place of prayer. They all received their food together after the period of fasting. No one drank any wine unless illness forced him to do so. Most of them were dressed in camel-skin garments: they considered the wearing of any softer material to be reprehensible. This is all the more remarkable since many of them were said to be noblemen

> who had been brought up in a very different way but had voluntarily adopted this life of humility and endurance. Later we saw several of them become bishops. For what city or church did not long to have a priest from Martin's monastery? (Severus c. 395:144)

Another important French monastic was John Cassian (*Jean Cassien*). Whereas Martin introduced monasticism to Gaul, Cassian was the first to give the western church written guidelines for the cenobitic life. Cassian was perhaps originally from Gaul, born around 360 of godly parents. As a young man, he joined a monastery in Bethlehem. During several long visits in Egypt, he interviewed many of the famous hermits and the best known of the monasteries. Around 400, he was active in the church at Constantinople under the leadership of John Chrysostom. When Chrysostom's zeal for reform ran into opposition from the political powers, Cassian was sent to Rome with a letter to the pope in Chrysostom's defense. Cassian then returned to Gaul and started a monastery in Marseilles (Douglas 1975:198).

Cassian's works, of which *The Institutes* is the most well known and influential, became the written rules for monasticism in the Western church. For Cassian, the purpose of the monastic life was the contemplation of God. This was to be accomplished through a fervent prayer life, the study of the Bible, a simple life style, and the fight against sin and temptation. All was to be done in a spirit of love, humility, moderation, and chastity. *The Institutes* would have a major influence on St. Benedict, and the Benedictine Rule would call for regular reading of Cassian's works (Douglas 1975:198).

Besides being a model for centuries of monks to follow, Cassian was also an example of Gallic independence. In *The Institutes*, he tries to defend a balanced view of grace and free will, particularly because he felt Augustine, who had all the favor of the pope, was putting too much emphasis on predestination. Cassian said that "some small and trivial efforts" were necessary, such as one's confession of sin or the placing of one's faith in Christ (c. 425:430). Pope Clementine I firmly, but with great respect, rebuked both him and those who sided with him (known as the School of Marseilles), but Cassian did not budge. After Cassian's death, he became more and more associated with semi-Pelagianism which was eventually condemned as a heresy. All though he never became a saint in the Roman church, his views would be quite acceptable in modern evangelical circles (Latourette 1975:181-182).

The Evangelization of Rural Areas

The Christianization of the rural parts of Gaul was slower than that of the cities. Up to the fourth century, the norm was to have one church per city which served a whole region. With the growth of Christianity, new branch churches were started in cities that already had a primary church. All of the new churches would still be under the leadership of the parent church's bishop. Certain bishops, of whom Martin is the foremost example, also evangelized the surrounding countryside. Martin was known for destroying pagan temples and sacred trees and for allegedly raising people from the dead in his evangelistic activities. He established churches in many rural areas, although in some cases these were little more than buildings with poorly trained priests assigned to teach a catechism and perform the ceremonies (Burnand 1996:104-105).

Martin's principal tool for evangelism was preaching. He would come to a town with a pagan shrine and start preaching the Gospel with the goal that the townsfolk would decide to destroy the shrine, construct a church, become catechumens, and eventually be baptized. However, sometimes he could not convince the locals to tear down their shrine, and he would do it himself. This of course led to some interesting conflicts and many parts of his famous biography by Severus explain what happened in these circumstances (Severus c. 395:146-48).

However, it seems like Severus tended to exaggerate and to describe the situations as he would have liked to see them happen. In Severus' work, the sign of the cross is often the key to effective evangelism. For example, the people of a town refused to let Martin chop down a sacred pine tree. Someone challenged him to let the tree fall on him as the townsfolk would chop down the tree. Martin accepted the challenge and was tied up and positioned according to where the tree would fall. As the tree was falling, Martin made the sign of the cross just before it landed on him. The tree was allegedly blown in another direction and almost landed on the townsfolk who were standing in a safe place (c. 395:147).

A recurrent theme in *The Life of Martin* is that Martin had "special power" that was not available to other Christians. The miracles of Martin are often quite different than the miracles of the Bible. For example, Martin one time thought he saw a pagan religious procession coming towards him. He made the sign of the cross at them and they miraculously froze like rocks. But when Martin realized that it was merely a funeral procession and that he had made a mistake, he raised his hand and granted them the power to start moving again (Severus c. 395:145-146).

A second form of rural evangelization resulted from the urban exodus provoked by the economic recession, the general cultural decline, and the barbarian invasions of the fourth and fifth centuries. The upper class left the decaying and vulnerable cities to move to the large farming centers (*les villas*) far outside the cities, bringing their Christianity with them. There, they would build fortifications and churches and replace the nearby pagan shrines (*les saints lieux*) with Christian ones. When surrounding rural folk (*paysans*) would then come to *les villas* for protection from barbarian invasions, they would be exposed to the Christian religious ceremonies and teaching (De Montclos 1988:25).

The evangelization (i.e. the ending of public observance of non-Christianized religious activities) of the rural areas was quite slow, not completed until at least the eighth century. The resistance of the rural areas can be seen in modern French, where "pagan" (*païen*) and "rural person" (*paysan*) share a common etymological origin (De Montclos 1988:26).

The Worship of Saints

Another phenomenon that developed during this period of history was the worship (*culte*) of saints. The rise of this practice can be understood on three levels. First of all, with the increase in worldliness in the church, for many the golden age of Christianity with its martyrs seemed to be over. Collecting the relics of these early witnesses seemed to be an appropriate way of assuring the continuity between the past and the present. Likewise, honoring the friends of God seemed like a good way to honor God himself (De Montclos 1988:13).

Secondly, the worship of saints was much more palatable to the polytheistic masses than the worship of an abstract, immaterial, transcendent God. It is commonly stated that the saints were the "successors of the gods" (De Montclos 1988:12).

These two tendencies often worked symbiotically. Sulpicius Severus, for example, an upper class Gallo-Roman and disciple and biographer of Martin of Tours, built at Primulac, near Béziers in the South-West of France, a small church for the body of Clair, another disciple of Martin and one of the last martyrs, killed while evangelizing in Aquitaine. He then imported from Italy relics from other martyrs and apostles from Italy, since Gaul had a relative scarcity of these. The people in the region felt that the presence of these relics would assure the continuation of the supernatural action that had been manifested in Martin's life. The promise that these bodies (or parts thereof) would one day come back to life also gave a concrete illustration of the resurrection. The curiosity and resulting worship of these relics were important factors leading to the mass conversion of the surrounding region (De Montclos 1988:12).

A third reason for the development of the worship of saints is that the practice produced a body of literature, both oral and written, which gave meaning and heroes to a civilization that faced desperate times. Beginning in the end of the fifth century, Gaul was decimated by a century of barbarian invasions, annihilating the Roman military and political presence. As the people helplessly watched their civilization crumble, the stories recounted by Severus and others gave them hope and heroes (De Montclos 1988:12).

Theological Innovations

By the middle of the fifth century, for the common person, Christianity consisted mainly of religious ceremonies and the veneration of holy places and relics. But within the monasteries and undoubtedly among many sincere believers, the content and the meaning of the Gospel were hotly debated. Several Gallic Christians made significant contributions to the theological debates of this epoch (De Montclos 1988:12, 14-16).

Some, like Hillary of Poitiers (the mentor of Martin of Tours), were quite orthodox and biblical. Hillary is especially known for his defense of Trinitarian orthodoxy after the Council of Milan in 355 led by the Arian-sympathizing Emperor Constantius. In 356, at the Council of Béziers, Hillary was exiled for his pro-Trinitarian convictions and his belief that the State should not intervene in ecclesiastical affairs. After the death of Constantius in 361, Hillary's banishment was lifted (Douglas 1975:470).

However, other Gallic monks tended to deviate from the biblical norms. One such deviation which became accepted during this time was the idea of baptismal regeneration. In the *Life of Martin*, Severus refuses to consider Martin a Christian before his baptism, even though he had faith in Christ and was living a holy life (c. 395:137). In another story, Severus tells of a catechumen who died before being baptized. God condemns him to hell, but two angels remind God that Martin was praying for him. God sends him back to earth and revives his body over which Martin is praying. Then the catechumen was immediately baptized in order to secure his salvation (c. 395:141).

Another important Gallic theologian is Vincent de Lérins who wrote in the first half of the fifth century. Lérins, an island off of modern day Cannes, was the site of an influential monastery which was closely linked to the church at Arles, the archbishop of which was considered the leading churchman of Gaul. Many important bishops came from this monastery who worked to protect the people from both the heresies and the social chaos that resulted from the barbarian invasions which were destroying what was left of the Roman state (Douglas 1975:1019-20).

Vincent de Lérins saw that, throughout the history of the church, much energy had been spent fighting heresies. He set up rules for differentiating between orthodoxy and heresy. The key, he felt, was understanding what the Scriptures taught. But unfortunately, he observed, the heretics also used Scripture to defend their teaching. So, one must distinguish between orthodoxy and heresy "first, by the authority of the Divine Law, and then, by the Tradition of the Catholic church."

> But here someone perhaps will ask, Since the canon of Scripture is complete, and sufficient of itself for everything, and more than sufficient, what need is there to join with it the authority of the Church's interpretation? For this reason, because, owing to the depth of Holy Scripture, all do not accept it in one and the same sense, but one understands its words in one way, another in another; so that it seems to be capable of as many interpretations as there are interpreters. For Novatian expounds it one way, Sabellius another, Donatus another, Arius, Eunomius, Macedonius, another. . .
>
> . . . in the Catholic church itself, all possible care must be taken that we hold that faith which has been believed everywhere, always, by all. For that is truly in the strictest sense "Catholic" . . . This rule we shall observe if we follow universality, antiquity, consent (Vincent de Lérins c. 435:132).

Vincent de Lérins thus gave a three-fold hermeneutic test for orthodoxy. The first element was universality (that which has been believed everywhere), the second was antiquity (that which has been believed always), and the third was consent (that which has been believed by all). If someone's teaching passed these three tests, it should be considered Catholic, i.e. orthodox.

Although he was personally rejected by much of the Catholic church because he tried to apply this test to Augustinian predestination, and thus brought upon himself the charge of semi-Pelagianism, his three-fold test became a major theme in French and all Roman church history. It would later (during the Council of Trent in the sixteenth century) be expanded into a doctrine which would place tradition on a par with biblical teaching, and since Scripture had to be interpreted in accordance with tradition, the practical effect would be to put tradition above Scripture (Latourette 1975:182, Douglas 1975:1019-20).

Missiological Applications

As we look back on this epoch, it is easy to classify it as one of decay and corruption because the content of the Gospel was diluted in order to accept the masses as Christians. But for a Christian in the fourth century, Constantine was a hero and the period that he heralded was a time of peace and relative stability. We should try to profit from the experiences of these Christians.

Assuring the Well Being of Our Congregations without Compromise

Missionaries who successfully start small churches often become, by necessity, pastors of these churches. Although they might not feel called to pastoral ministries, as soon as small flocks are gathered, these missionaries will sense the people's need for shepherding and will want to respond to it. This often involves comforting and welcoming people who are far from the Gospel, in both belief and lifestyle. The missionary will want to show Christ's love to these people and create an atmosphere where these people are loved and accepted. However, the missionary-pastor must lead the church without compromising Biblical standards. The bishops of the fourth century were rightfully joyous that the persecutions ended and their church members would be left in peace. Yet the door was open to non-believers coming into the church as Christianity became the only legal form of religion. Perhaps at the beginning it seemed like a small price to pay for tranquility, but as those who were far from the gospel gained influence, it resulted in a perversion of the true Gospel, often difficult to rediscover before the Reformation. The missionary pastors of today must make sure that they, in their desire to love and accept others, do not allow seeds of corruption to enter into their ministry.

For example, to be legally constituted as a church, there needs to be a certain number of members depending on the size of the city where the incorporation takes place. To reach this number of people and the resulting blessings, it can be quite tempting to allow people to become members who express their faith in only ambiguous terms. Undoubtedly, in certain cases this would be acceptable, but members who are ambivalent in their faith only weaken the church in the long run. Similarly, there might be pressure from families to baptize their children before they are of an age (often considered in the French evangelical world to be the late teens) when they can make a truly personal profession of faith. These situations must be faced with sensitivity, love, and a strong commitment to Biblical teaching.

The Importance of Cultural Integration

One of the reasons that Christianity was legalized and later adopted as the state religion was because the intellectuals of the epoch found it a welcome and realistic alternative to other forms of philosophic and religious expression. If we want biblical Christianity to have the same effect on France today, we need to be presenting it to the intellectuals as a viable alternative to contemporary philosophies. This is not easy when the church is limited to foreigners, the unstable, and the uneducated. Therefore, a missionary, in order to maximize his or her impact on France, needs to make sure he or she does not miss any opportunities to share the Gospel with people who have the potential to be the movers and shakers of society. It is especially important that those with the necessary intellectual and social skills develop their gifts as leaders. Missionaries must make this one of their top priorities.

Purity of Worship

As the churches became more and more like centers for religious expression rather than assemblies of genuinely converted disciples of Jesus Christ, those who sincerely tried to follow Christ could not be satisfied with the worship, the fellowship, and the opportunities for service that the local churches offered. They felt the need to form their own communities which would cut them off from the worldliness of the churches. In the churches that we start, we need to make sure that this does not happen.

We need to be on our guard to make sure that the assemblies that we found as church planters stay truly Christian and dynamic in their worship, fellowship, and service. They must be communities where the truly converted feel they are part of the community of the redeemed and that they can freely express their love for Christ. We must avoid an atmosphere in the church where it is more important to be non-offensive than to be faithful to the Gospel. If we seek to cater to non-Christians so much that the stumbling block of the cross is removed, we have gone too far and are making disciples of ourselves and not of Jesus Christ. Certainly, we must be "seeker sensitive" and make the church as friendly to non-Christians as possible, but if there is little "solid food" (I Cor. 3:2) presented, the genuine Christian will die of malnutrition. If the relationships between the people remain superficial, there will be no true Christian fellowship which will enable them to grow in their love for and service to Christ.

Evangelization of the Most Receptive

We see that already in the third and fourth centuries that certain people were easier to evangelize than others; notably those in the cities were more receptive. Undoubtedly, this was because they were more cosmopolitan and open to new ideas, as well as the fact that ideas could travel faster among more people in an urban setting.

Among the French today, it is difficult to say what part of the population is the most receptive (undoubtedly the non-French!). But it seems likely that urban and suburban areas will be slightly more open than the traditional rural areas for the same reasons as were true during Roman times.

However, even in the city, the number of people open to new ideas (especially concerning Christianity) is highly limited and the communication network of the majority of those who convert is also often quite restrained. This means that the missionary will want to have contact with as many people as possible in culturally sensitive ways to find those who are possibly open to the Gospel; this can be done

The Beginning of Christianity as the State Religion

relatively inexpensively through attractive mass mailings or other forms of advertising. In this way, those in whom God is already at work can contact the church themselves. The missionary will also need to make it a priority to give extra encouragement and training to Christians to try to share their faith in their natural networks, since if they have few friends, they might fear losing them by talking about a subject as unpopular as the Gospel.

Profiting from the Urban Exodus

In the fourth and fifth centuries the population fled from cities to the *villas* and the surrounding countryside for protection from the decay and danger that threatened them in the cities. At the beginning of the twenty-first century, there is a similar urban exodus each week-end as Parisians flee the city seeking peace and security from the decay and danger that threatens them there. In fact, the worst traffic congestion of the week in the Paris area occurs on Sunday evenings as everyone is returning.

An effective tool (relatively speaking) in evangelism is the church week-end retreat since leaving the city for a week-end responds to a genuine felt need. Not only do such week-ends help bond a community of believers, but it also gives non-Christians the possibility to observe Christians in action in a relaxed situation (relaxed at least from the point of view of those who are not organizing the week-end).

The fact that Parisians like going out of town for the week-end is effectively used by other religions. The Catholics, the New Age cults, and especially the Buddhist movements all organize retreats which are for many of the participants the only religious activities in their lives. The openness to this sort of activity must not be overlooked.

The Importance of Visual Aids

One of the reasons that the masses were attracted to the relics and tombs of the saints is that they were so visual and they stimulated the imagination of those coming to see them. It is highly likely that the teaching that occurred where the relics were located was probably orthodox, at least at the beginning, but the message communicated by the visual was much louder and was therefore the one that the masses retained.

We, too, need to use visual aids to better teach those for whom we have responsibility, but we need to make sure that the message taught by our visuals corresponds to the biblical message. For example, if all one sees when he or she comes to an evangelical church is a building in need of renovation, a few faded posters, and group of poorly dressed individuals, it will be difficult for him or her to retain the evangelical message of newness in Christ. However, if he or she sees friendly, smiling faces while entering, and, during the message, a clear outline on a screen of what the pastor is trying to say, accompanied by, for example, a caterpillar that the pastor's son caught and put in a bottle, the message of the new birth will stick with him or her a little better.

A Balanced View of Baptism

For centuries, the Roman church has taught that baptism is necessary for salvation. Evangelicals have long rejected this doctrine for biblical reasons, but sometimes at the risk of underemphasizing the biblical teaching on baptism. Many North American missionaries, including those from even Baptist churches, come from a milieu in which the baptism of children is the norm. This is usually not the case in established, evangelical churches in France, apart from some of the Reformed [*réformées*] churches which are still within the evangelical current. Adult baptism is the norm and even those who grow up in the faith are encouraged to wait until the late teens, after the *crise d'adolescence,* to be baptized, in order to see if their faith is sincere.

Baptisms are usually performed at a special worship service, often on Sunday afternoons after a shared meal (*repas fraternal*). Because it is often the most visible and tangible sign associated with a person's placing his or her faith in Christ, many Christians very closely link their baptism with their conversion. They would have no problem agreeing with Peter that "baptism now saves you—not the removal of dirt from the flesh but an appeal to God for a good conscience—through the resurrection of Jesus Christ" (I Pet. 3:21).

Clear Hermeneutics

Because Vincent de Lérins' three-fold test for orthodoxy (that which has been believed everywhere, always, and by all) is beyond the capacity of the average person to apply, and because the Catholic church discouraged personal Bible reading up until the 1960s, many people believe that they are incapable of understanding the Bible. It is common to hear people say that since there are so many ways to interpret the Bible, reading it is not especially useful. The missionary needs to explain that a person most likely can understand the Bible and probably interpret it correctly. The missionary needs to teach a clear hermeneutic that takes into account the historical, cultural, and literary context of the passage in question. The missionary will most likely find that this type of analysis is quite acceptable in the French world-view because it is exactly the type of literary analysis that the French school system teaches them to do.

54

4
The Merovingian Church: The Fifth through Seventh Centuries

A great many things keep happening, some of them good, some of them bad. The inhabitants of different countries keep quarreling fiercely with each other and kings go on losing their temper in the most furious way. Our churches are attacked by the heretics and then protected by the Catholics; the faith of Christ burns bright in many men, but it remains lukewarm in others (Gregory of Tours 591:63).

The time known as the Early Middle Ages, the time of the Merovingian kings (the Frankish kings who descended from a common ancestor, the king Mérovée, d. 458), is perhaps the least familiar epoch of Western history for both the North American missionary and the French in general. But

56   THE RELIGIOUS HISTORY OF FRANCE

this period is rich in institutional developments within the Catholic church. As Gaul became France, the cultural identity of the inhabitants changed immensely and became more and more linked to the new forms of Christianity (Frémy and Frémy 1986:603).

The Barbarian Invasions

Beginning in the middle of the fourth century, various barbarian tribes began invading Gaul. The Roman army had grown too weak to defend the western part of the Empire, so the Roman administration negotiated treaties with the barbarians which granted them the right to settle within Roman territory, under the Roman administration, with the title *fédéré* in return for collaborating (theoretically) with the Romans to defend the Empire. Since many barbarians were completely ignorant of Roman culture and many individuals kept their tribal customs and religions, this cohabitation was tense and filled with conflicts (Rivière 1986:20-22).

The Franks

In the early fifth century, Gaul was ravaged by several particularly vicious waves of invasions and the Roman administrative presence dwindled. By the middle of the century, many areas were completely controlled by various tribes. In 476 there was no longer an emperor of the Western Empire when the Roman Empire was theoretically united with Constantinople as its capital. In 486, the Franks, under the leadership of their king Clovis, defeated the last Roman army in the Western Empire, at Soissons, north of Paris, transforming much of Roman Gaul into the Land of the Franks, later known as France (Rivière 1986:22).

The history of the Franks before Clovis is unclear. They, like the other invading tribes, were war-loving people perhaps originating in the Nordic countries. By 250 A.D. they had settled on the German side of the Rhine River. Their first penetration into Gaul was around 430. Like the Anglo-Saxons who invaded Brittany, they were still pagan at the time of the Fall of Rome. The worship of woodland and water animals in the form of statues played a major role in their religion (Rey 1987:678).

Other Invading Tribes

The Franks, however, were far from being the only Germanic people vying for power in Gaul. Before the fall of Rome, each tribe would seek Roman titles and in some way or another viewed themselves as members of the Empire. However, the reality of the matter was that each tribe developed its own more or less independent kingdom (Rivière 1986:21).

In Gaul, the Visigoths (Western Goths) eventually controlled Aquitaine (South-West France) and Spain. The Ostrogoths (Eastern Goths) controlled the extreme southern part of France and much of Italy. The Burgundians settled in the eastern side of Central and Southern France as well as in Switzerland. All of these invading tribes eventually considered themselves more or less Christians. The Goths, however were Arian Christians and there was a strong Arian element present in the Burgundian church as well. This was a source of tension between the Gallic and Roman subjects who were loyal to Roman and Nicean Christianity and their political dominators who were loyal to the heretical form of Christianity (Rey 1987:747).

The Gauls tended to mix little with these invaders. The two communities, Roman and barbarian, had separate cultures and administrative structures, with the barbarian kings holding the final authority (because of their military might) within the context of Roman style law. The differences between Nicean and Arian Christianity also separated the communities (Rivière 1986:20-21).

The Huns and the Vandals also invaded Gaul in the fifth century. They were the source of much destruction and suffering, but they established no kingdoms in what is now France (Rey 1987:867, 1841).

The Role of the Bishops

During the most horrible epochs of the barbarian invasions, the bishops played a very important role in society. Since Rome was no longer capable of providing minimal protection to the people, the church (led by the bishops), did all it could to meet the needs. The bishops would help organize and support military resistance, negotiate with the barbarians, and help the wounded and hunger-stricken. They became the primary representatives and defenders of both Christianity and Roman culture (including such elements as reading, writing, and the Roman style of administration) (De Montclos 1988:18-19).

Because of the role they played in society, the status of the bishops in the eyes of the common people grew immensely. They became viewed more and more as the protectors of the people and the defenders of peace and culture. Even in the eyes of the invading barbarians, they often received respect. The invaders could recognize the bishops' educational superiority as well as the influence that they exerted upon the population. Thus both the invaders and the defeated masses recognized and thus reinforced the authority of the bishops and the church (De Montclos 1988:18-19).

One quite important example of an influential bishop of this epoch was Germanus (*Germain*) of Auxerre (c. 370-448). He came from a rich Roman family, studied law at Autun and Rome, became a lawyer and then a government official and, in 418, was asked to become bishop of his native city. During his ministry, he built several large churches, organized several monasteries, and was sent by the pope to Great Britain to teach against Pelagianism. He also encouraged Geneviève to become a nun, who later was credited with protecting Paris by her prayers during the invasion of Attila the Hun. Near the end of his life, he risked his own life during a minor uprising to protect local peasants from the the Alans, a minor barbarian tribe with origins in Iran. The king of the Alans had been sent by Rome to squash the rebellion. Germanus dissuaded the king who withdrew from attacking. Germanus then went to Italy to plead for the pardon of those who had rebelled, thus gaining a glorious reputation as the protector of the people (De Montclos 1988:18).

The Conversion of the Franks

Since the Franks were pagan and most of the other barbarian tribes were Christian (at least in name) at the end of the fifth century, it seemed unlikely that they would eventually become the principal defenders of Roman Catholic orthodoxy and culture. However, this is exactly what happened.

The Baptism of Clovis

Clovis, son of Childeric I was born around 466. In 481 he became king of one part of the Franks and inherited a small kingdom, as Frankish kings sometimes divided their kingdom among their sons. He was a great warrior and general and his kingdom grew with his military conquests. Before his thirtieth birthday, he brought all the other Franks under his control, defeated the last Roman army in Gaul, and conquered the Alamanni, another pagan tribe which had settled in what is now Southern Germany (Rey 1987:421).

Clovis' first recorded contact with the church came around the time he defeated the Roman army. This event would become part of French mythology, defining a model for church and state interaction. Like all barbarian invaders, Clovis and the Franks would pillage the churches in the cities that they conquered. After pillaging the church in Soissons, the bishop sent a message to Clovis asking him, even if he would give nothing else back, if it might be possible to have one especially treasured vessel back (Gregory of Tours 591:139-140).

Clovis responded that it might be possible, if he could obtain it. The booty had not yet been divided by lot, so Clovis went to Soissons to see what he could do. Clovis asked all his men if he could have the vessel in question, and all but one man responded yes to show their loyalty to the king. One man voted no, saying that the booty should be divided up by the traditional and legal way. Nevertheless, Clovis took the vessel and returned it to the bishop. Later, when Clovis was inspecting his troops, he came across the man who had voted no. Clovis started to inspect the man's weapons. He picked up the man's ax, saying it was in horrible condition, and threw it to the ground. When the soldier bent over to pick it up, Clovis took his own ax and split the man's head with it. This story illustrates the assumed rights and responsibilities of both the church and the state, as well as the consequences for breaking with the expected roles. This model, where the Church could expect (but not demand) help from the State, was followed up to the time of the Revolution (Gregory of Tours 591:139-140).

Burgundy did not come under the control of the Franks during Clovis' lifetime. However, some of his envoys discovered there a young niece of the king who was beautiful, elegant, and intelligent. The envoys brought news of this girl, Clotilda (*Clotilde*), to Clovis and he asked her uncle for her hand in marriage. Clotilda was a committed, orthodox Christian, and soon became the favorite wife of Clovis (Gregory of Tours 591:141).

Tradition indicates that Clotilda witnessed to her husband continually. Her principal argument was that the pagan idols and the Roman gods that Clovis worshiped were immoral and powerless. The Christian God, however, was all powerful and the Creator of the universe. Clovis could not be persuaded that the Christian God existed, but he allowed their first son to be baptized (Gregory of Tours 591:141).

Clotilda thought the baptismal ceremony might be the chance to lead her husband to faith in God. "She ordered the church to be decorated with hangings and curtains, in the hope that the King, who remained stubborn in the face of argument, might be brought to faith by ceremony" (Gregory of Tours 591:142). But soon afterwards, the child died, hardening Clovis' heart even more to Christianity. Clovis was furious, blaming God for the child's death, but Clotilda remained faithful to God, counting it an honor to have born a child that was able to be baptized and receive eternal life.

Clotilda and Clovis had a second child, and soon after his baptism, he, too, fell sick. Clovis felt this was the curse of the gods upon him, but Clotilda prayed, and the child recovered. Clotilda continued to pray for the conversion of her husband (Gregory of Tours 591:141).

When war started with the Alamanni, the Franks were suffering important losses. In one battle, it looked like Clovis' army was going down to sure defeat. He saw that his gods were doing him no good, so Clovis prayed to Christ, promising to believe in him and be baptized if he would help him win the battle. As soon as he finished praying, the Franks started winning and finally came out victorious. When Clovis came home, he told Clotilda all that happened (Gregory of Tours 591:143-44).

Upon hearing this, Clotilda summoned Rémi, the bishop of Reims famed for his great learning, and pleaded with him to meet with the king and share the Gospel with him. The bishop agreed, and met with Clovis. Clovis said he was willing to convert, but only if his army would do so also, forsaking their traditional gods. Clovis met with his army, and they agreed to turn to the God of the Christians. A magnificent baptismal service was organized, and the king was baptized first, followed by 3000 of his army. When Rémi baptized Clovis on Christmas in 496, he told the king the now familiar "Bow your head in humility, . . . worship what you have burned, burn what you have worshiped" (Rey 1987:1508).

Thus the dominant power in Western Europe adopted Roman Christianity, the first nation to do so after the disintegration of the Empire. This event is sometimes called the baptism of France and for this reason, France is called the eldest daughter of the church (Frémy and Frémy 1998:508).

The Merovingian Influence on the Church

Although it is impossible to discern all the motives that led to the conversion of Clovis, one was probably the desire to profit from the close relationship that the bishops had with the

The Merovingian Church

people. If Clovis and the Franks really wanted to govern the Romanized Gauls, they needed to have the support of the bishops. Likewise, the Catholic Gauls needed the Franks to protect them from the Arian Goths and Burgundians. In 534, Clovis defeated the Burgundians and imposed Roman Christianity upon them; in 585, the Arian Goths in Spain and South-West France converted to Roman Christianity because their Catholic King wanted religious unity. The Goths in Gaul were later conquered by the Franks (De Montclos 1988:21).

Because the Romanized Gauls and the Franks now shared the same religion, this encouraged the mixture of the two peoples through marriage. The kings freely consulted with the bishops, and non-Franks were frequently given positions of authority. By the middle of the eighth century, at the end of the Merovingian dynasty, the ethnic identities of the two people were practically obliterated (Rivière 1987:23-25).

However, the Frankish kings turned out to be far from model Christians. What stands out about them in the French history of this epoch is their extreme love for violence. Gregory of Tours, in his conclusion on the life of Clovis tells the following story:

> One day when he had called a general assembly of his subjects, he is said to have made the following remark about the relatives whom he had destroyed: 'How sad a thing it is that I live among strangers like some solitary pilgrim, and that I have none of my own relations left to help me when disaster threatens!' He said this not because he grieved for their deaths, but because in his cunning way he hoped to find some relative still in the land of the living whom he could kill (591:158).

One of the main reasons for this violence was the Frankish tradition of dividing a king's domain among the princes upon his death. This naturally led to a competition among the princes and other relatives to defeat one another in order to gain control of a kingdom which was frequently divided. Thus, through a process of natural selection, the most powerful kings were those who were the most bloodthirsty and merciless. Some of the kings, though all nominally Christian, scoffed at God. For example, Gregory of Tours tells the following story of Lothar I, the son of Clovis:

> In the fifty-first year of his reign, while he was hunting in the forest of Cuise, he fell ill with a high temperature and took to his bed in his villa in Compiègne. There he lay, suffering from a high fever. 'Well! Would you believe it?' he asked. 'What manner of King can be in charge of heaven, if he is prepared to finish off great monarchs like me in this fashion?' While he was in the agony of his spirit, he died (591:217).

Since many Merovingian kings were willing to do anything to secure their power, it was natural for them to use the church in any way that they could to accomplish their goals. One of the most natural ways to do this, and a practice that would last for over a millennium, was to appoint bishops. Up to this point, it was normally the priests and the community leaders who would choose a new bishop upon the death of the bishop previously over them. This decision would be ratified by the surrounding bishops. But when the kings became involved in the process, they would use threats of violence or economic persecution if the person of their choosing was not appointed to the bishopric, obtaining the power and prestige associated with it. The atmosphere was ripe for moral decay to run rampant. A bishop that Lothar I appointed, for example, wanted a certain man in his diocese to cede certain property to the church. The man refused, so the bishop had him buried alive. The kings also saw the churches as a source of tax revenues, and up to a third of the income that the church received from various sources had to be paid to the king (Gregory of Tours 591:200-10).

Another use that the Merovingian kings found for the church was as a prison for their enemies. Clovis, for example, captured one of the rival Frankish kings and this king's son. He had their long hair, the sign of royalty, cut short and had the father ordained as a priest and made his son a deacon. At another time, King Guntram, son of Lothar I, learned that one of his brothers had died. He asked his brothers' widow to marry him and she consented. But immediately after the marriage, Guntram confiscated his dead brother's wealth and had his new bride made a nun. She secretly made contact with a Goth who promised to carry her off to Spain and marry her there. The story ends as follows:

> As she was about to make her escape from the nunnery, she was surprised by the vigilant abbess. The abbess, who had caught her red-handed, had her beaten mercilessly and locked her up in her cell. There she remained until her dying day, suffering awful anguish (Gregory of Tours 591:221).

But not all of the Merovingian monarchs were evil, nominal Christians who abused their power. Queen Clotilda, after the death of her husband Clovis, continued to seek God and do what she could for his glory. She remained chaste, gave money to the poor, spent time praying every day, and endowed many churches and monasteries with the land necessary to insure their upkeep. "Already in her lifetime she was looked upon not as a Queen but as the handmaiden of God whom she served with such zeal" (Gregory of Tours 591:182). Many other rich people left large parts of their estates to churches or monasteries, either because of a love for God or a desire to secure their eternal destiny.

Piety among the Merovingians was expressed in other ways as well. King Theudebert, a grandson of Clovis, was known as a good king, in spite of having a marital life that was far from being exemplary:

> Once he was firmly established on the throne, Theudebert proved himself to be a great king, distinguished by every virtue. He ruled his kingdom justly, respected the bishops, was liberal to the churches, relieved the wants of the poor and distributed many benefits with piety and friendly goodwill (Gregory of Tours 591:185).

Another prince, Chlodovald (*St. Cloud*), devoted himself completely to God. He gave up his royal rights, as was expected for one wishing to serve Christ, and joined a monastery outside of Paris, in a town which is now named after him (Gregory of Tours 591:182).

Although there were some sincere, God-fearing Merovingians, for the most part, these kings and princes were far from ideal Christians. This weakened the church because it encouraged compromise. Gregory of Tours cites the example of how he knew he should not give communion to a wicked king, but "Merovech threatened to kill some of our congregation if he were not allowed to take communion with us" (591:268). All things considered, Gregory thought it more important to protect his flock than to demand purity within the church.

The churches were also weakened because of Merovingian ruthlessness and the corrupt bishops that the kings appointed. Gregory of Tours describes the Christians at the end of the sixth century:

> We can only contrast how their forefathers used to behave with how they themselves are behaving today. After the missionary preaching of the bishops, the earlier generations were converted from their pagan temples and turned towards the churches; now they are busy plundering those same churches. The older folk listened with all their heart to the Lord's bishops and had great reverence for them; nowadays they not only do not listen, but they persecute instead. Their forefathers endowed the monasteries and churches; the sons tear them to pieces and demolish them (591:244).

Ecclesiastical and Theological Advances

Although the fifth through eighth centuries were some of the darkest in the history of Western Civilization, God was still at work and many positive things occurred. The Western (Roman or Nicean) church evolved in both ecclesiastical structure and theological understanding of God and the world. Not all of this evolution was positive, but many of the foundations were laid for today's Catholic Church in France.

Cultural Regression

Beginning in the fifth and sixth centuries, the *régression culturelle* that had begun in the third century began to accelerate. This was seen in the economic decline of the cities, the urban exodus, and especially the loss of the Greek and Roman forms of expression, such as writing, reading and the arts. As the classic schools disappeared, oral tradition became the primary way of passing information from one generation to another. The principal factors shaping one's education became the rural folklore of Gaul and the military folklore of the Franks. In the fifth and sixth centuries, this decline was most marked in the North of France, but by the seventh century, there were no more schools in the South of France either (Rivière 1987:24-25).

The church, as well as individual aristocratic families, tried to hold on to Greek and Roman culture, but was only half able to do so, and the little that was being written was of mediocre quality. This lack of writing is what motivated Gregory of Tours to write his *History of the Franks*:

> In fact in the towns of Gaul the writing of literature has declined to the point where it has virtually disappeared altogether. Many people have complained about this, not once but time and time again. 'What a poor period this is!' they have been heard to say. 'If among all our people there is not one man to be found who can write a book about what is happening today, the pursuit of letters really is dead in us!' (591:63).

The Evangelization of France

Since Christianity was primarily the religion of a Book, the cultural decline and the urban exodus of the epoch made a fruitful field for the resurgence of pagan beliefs. Evangelism was always a priority for the bishops who sought to be faithful. Even as the cities were shrinking, the churches were growing. Gregory of Tours describes two churches built in the fifth century, in Tours and Clermont-Ferrand, which is our first description of Gallic "mega-churches," churches which by today's standards would seat over a thousand or have standing room for over two thousand (591:130-131).

The Merovingian Church

In the church records of this epoch, we see that evangelism of the rural masses was a theme that was quite important to the bishops. Of special concern was the need to simplify the message so that it would be understandable to the common person. Césaire, bishop of Arles in the first half of the sixth century, is to have said, "I humbly ask the ears of the literate to be content to endure, without complaining, rustic expressions, in order that the Lord's flock might receive heavenly food in a simple and down to earth language" (in De Montclos 1988:23).

Another concern was with the priests who were responsible for the many small rural churches. Many of them were simple people, not trained in theology or preaching, principally practicing ceremonies in the church, not capable of communicating the message of the Gospel to others, perhaps not even understanding it. Many priests were almost as steeped in pagan superstition as were the people they worked with. Eloi, bishop of Noyon in the seventh century, is said to have preached, "No Christian must ever put an amulet on the neck of a man or an animal, even if it was given to him by the clergy" (De Montclos 1988:24).

One of the most popular manifestations of Christianity was the procession of Rogations, a religious festival with a parade, usually taking place on the three days before Ascension, usually in May. Instituted by Mamert, bishop of Vienne, in 474 to replace pagan sun worshiping rites, by the sixth century, it was soon celebrated all over France. The purpose of the procession was to seek divine blessing on the recently planted crops. The procession often included carrying a saint's relics or statue around town. These processions are still practiced in many places today, and everywhere in France the month of May is unique among all the months because there are so many religious and secular legal holidays (De Montclos 1988:23).

Preaching and teaching were perhaps the greatest elements that were lacking in the many churches of this epoch. Without an evangelical message, churches often became centers for mere religious ceremonies and Christianized folklore where one might learn more about a saint than about God. As we shall see later, it was principally in the monasteries that Christian teaching was preserved, and the monks themselves also played a major role in the evangelization of France (De Montclos 1988:24).

The Fight against Arianism

The other great combat in France, besides against paganism, was against Arianism, the heresy which denied the deity of Christ and the Trinity, teaching instead that Christ was a created being. Although condemned by several Councils in the fourth century, it was still the religion of the Goths in the western part of Gaul and was very present in Burgundy until the sixth century. Since Clovis's conversion in 496, the Franks were Catholic, so it was natural for the church to support the Franks' wars against their heretical neighbors who often persecuted the Catholics. By 536, both the Burgundians and the Goths of Gaul were subjected to the Merovingians and Catholic Christianity (Douglas 1978:67-68).

It is difficult to tell how widespread the heresy was after the sixth century, but quite often we find Gregory of Tours assuring the reader that he really is Catholic. The introduction of his *History of the Franks* is a confession of faith that leaves no doubt that he is Catholic and not Arian (591:67). Throughout his book he tells of how Christians had been persecuted by Arians, how God had been with the

The Merovingian Church 71

Merovingians as they defeated the Arians, and why one should reject Arian doctrines.

While some of Gregory's arguments against Arianism are not likely to be used by modern evangelicals (for example, the fact that Arius died while on the toilet, thus showing God's displeasure with him), others are exactly the same arguments that we would use today. He cites John 10:30, "I and my Father are one," John 1:1, "In the beginning was the Word," and Acts 5:3-4, "Why . . . did you lie to the Holy Spirit? You did not lie to man, but to God." He also used several metaphysical arguments to argue for the unity of the Trinity, which go beyond the interest of most people of today (591:307-309).

Without a doubt, the greatest good achieved by the Merovingian church, from a later medieval point of view, was the unification of Gaul under Catholicism (De Montclos 1987:20-21). In fact, Catholicism would hold France together for more than a millennium.

Theological Innovations

This was not a time of great theological development. However, there were several novelties and innovations that have had a drastic impact on the religious history of France.

In 529, the second Council of Orange, in the South of France, was convened to decide what stance to take on semi-Pelagianism (or semi-Augustinianism). The majority of monasteries in France, including Lérins, led by Faustus of Riez, sided with the teachings found in Faustus' writings, as well as the writings of Vincent de Lérins and John Cassian which were considered semi-Pelagian. However, under the presidency of Césaire of Arles, the bishops condemned these semi-Pelagian writings and created a statement on grace and free will (Latourette 1975:182).

The Canons of the Council of Orange were good in as much as they emphasized the need for grace and they condemned the idea that man was predestined to evil. They clearly taught that no one could come to faith in Christ apart from grace. However, the condition for obtaining this grace was baptism. "The freedom of will that was destroyed in the first man can be restored only by the grace of baptism" (Césaire of Arles 529:Canon 12). "After grace has been received through baptism, all baptized persons have the ability and responsibility, if they desire to labor faithfully, to perform with the aid and cooperation of Christ what is of essential importance in regard to the salvation of their soul" (Césaire of Arles 529:Canon 25).

The evangelical message of Christ's salvation being available only by God's grace through faith was thus transformed into the message that if one is baptized, he or she can strive to have the faith and works necessary for salvation. Pope Boniface II approved *The Canons of the Council of Orange* in 531, thus making baptism the key event necessary for salvation. Thus the question of personal conversion, the decision to put one's faith in Christ and the resulting transformation by the Holy Spirit, was relegated to a secondary position (Latourette 1975:182).

This, of course, helped justify the baptism and Christianization of the masses, people in whom no sign of supernatural transformation could be seen. This view of baptism became the official view held by the French church, forever confusing the question of how one obtains salvation (Latourette 1975:351).

Gregory the Great, pope from 590 to 604, did much to establish Roman authority over the church in Gaul. Gregory was the principal religious and political leader in Italy at the time, but his influence spread much farther (Douglas 1978:432).

From at least the second century, the church in Rome held a special place among the churches. Since Rome was the cultural and political center of the world, it was natural that the church there would be the home of the best and the brightest, holding a position of special prestige in the eyes of the other churches, especially of those in the Western Empire. The fact that Rome made the most reliable claims to having the relics of Peter and Paul added to its prestige (Eusebius 324:150-151).

But up to the end of the sixth century, the church of Gaul was essentially independent of Rome. The bishops up to this time would have wanted to know what Rome's opinion was in all that touched the faith, but essentially the bishops were free to do what they wanted (Latourette 1975:336-37).

Like other Roman bishops before him, Gregory made claims that Rome's authority extended over the other churches. But for the first time in Gaul, this message began to meet a felt need. The Merovingian church was in such sorry shape that the idea of leadership coming from outside of Gaul seemed attractive to those who wanted to see reform in the church. Gregory was successful in establishing a vicar (a person acting as a liaison to represent Rome's authority) in Gaul. This, in theory, brought the Frankish church partly under Rome's direction. Gregory took other steps to establish his authority in England, Germany, and Spain as well (Latourette 1975:336-41).

Gregory was a great leader both of the Italian church and of the churches farther away. He was a prolific writer, his most influential work being *A Pastoral Rule* (*Règle Pastoral*) which was used throughout the Middle Ages as a training guide for priests. He wanted the clergy to be disciplined, and sought to enforce the policy of mandatory celibacy for priests. He wrote on many topics that reflected the popular theology of the sixth century. Some of his most influential teaching concerned purgatory (Latourette 1975:340-41).

He agreed with the Council of Orange's idea that original sin was erased at baptism. But sins committed after baptism required repentance, penitence and contrition in order to be forgiven. Those sins that did not have the required amount of penitence would be punished in purgatory, an intermediate state that Christians would pass through before going to the final judgment. Suffering in purgatory could also be reduced by masses being performed and by seeking the aid of saints (Latourette 1975:340).

Undoubtedly, the motivation behind this teaching was to encourage Christians to act like Christians. But, in reality, it was interpreted by the common person as a form of universalism. Since virtually everyone was baptized (except the soon to arrive neo-pagans, the Muslims), everyone could be assured that they would make it to heaven after a little suffering in purgatory.

The Monasteries during the Time of the Merovingians

The trend towards monasticism which gathered momentum in the fourth century continued during the Merovingian period. It was the normal way to express a sincere and profound commitment to Christ. But just as the number of problems within the churches grew during this period, so did the number of monasteries and the problems that they faced.

External Influences on the Frankish Monasteries

As Western culture crumbled throughout Gaul, many people, educated and uneducated, turned to monasticism in order to find a more structured, stable, and Christ-centered lifestyle. Though there were few original Frankish or Latin thinkers in Gaul at this time, the monasteries in Gaul underwent great transformations during this period of history, primarily due to foreign influences, coming from both the North and the South (De Montclos 1988:26-27).

From the North, traveling Irish monks started to come to Gaul. Ireland had been spared much of the suffering that resulted from the barbarian invasions, leaving the remains of Roman civilization less weakened than on the continent. The Irish church used Latin, but was still independent of Rome, though doctrinally in agreement. The Irish Christians expressed their commitment to Christ in a very rigorous form of monasticism. In Ireland, there was no system of bishops and dioceses organized as a parallel to civil government; Christianity was organized around the monasteries (Latourette 1975:322-23).

In the sixth century, many Irish monks began immigrating to other countries, more or less doing missionary work. Some lived as hermits or in small communities that had little influence on the people among whom they lived. But others were very effective missionaries, both in converting those who were still pagan and in giving moral instruction to those who were already baptized (Latourette 1975:322-23).

Since they were not part of the established church of Gaul, they were often a source of irritation to the bishops. They did not have a place in the administrative structure of the Gallic churches and they would act independently of the bishops attached to the Roman church, choosing themselves whom they would ordain. They continued to immigrate to the continent and influence the Kingdom of the Franks and Charlemagne's Empire until well into the tenth century (Latourette 1975:343).

The most influential of the traveling Irish monks that came to Gaul was Columban (or Columbanus, *Columban*). Like Christ with his twelve apostles, Columban and his twelve monks arrived in Gaul around 598. They settled in the Vosges region with the approval of one of the Frankish kings. Columban quickly made enemies with the local bishop because of his zeal, his extreme asceticism, his habit of celebrating Easter on a different date, and his general indifference to the already existing church structure. He started a soon to be famous monastery in Luxeuil. He was very popular with the local population. Since he was highly educated and could study the Scriptures in both Greek and Hebrew, his monastery became an intellectual center. However, opposition to his ministry increased when he rebuked the king for polygamy. Finally he had to flee Frankish lands to save his life. However, many of his disciples stayed in France and continued a similar ministry of evangelism and starting monasteries (Latourette 1975:342-43).

A second influence on Frankish monasteries came from the South, in Italy, where Benedict of Nursia (*Benoît de Nursie*) had used his administrative genius in setting up rules for his monastery. In 529 he established a monastery at Monte Cassino, halfway between Rome and Naples in the South of Italy. His rules show that he was familiar with John Cassian and other famous monks. But his rule, known as the Benedictine Rule, went much further: It organized the monk's entire day and his whole life. After passing through a one year apprentice period, the monk would make an irrevocable commitment to the order for the rest of his life. The rule

The Merovingian Church   77

especially emphasized poverty (the monks were not allowed to own any possessions), chastity, and obedience to the abbot (Latourette 1975:333-36).

In the second half of the sixth century, Benedictine monasteries began to multiply. Pope Gregory the Great was himself a Benedictine. The monasteries were to be self-supporting with their own fields and work areas, and were to owe nothing to those outside the community, even if someone gave a large gift to the monastery. The model for the monastery was the Jerusalem church, where all gave their possessions to the community and had no claim that anything was his own. This goal of seeking the common good for the community turned out to be an important source of multi-generational stability (Latourette 1975:333-36).

In the second half of the seventh century, the Benedictine Rule gained popularity in Gaul. Life under the Benedictine Rule was more flexible and less strict than under the rules established by Columban. The monasteries were not especially geared toward evangelism and their primary contact with the world was to draw new members towards themselves. There was a close link between the Benedictines and the Pope, and this helped the monasteries integrate into the local ecclesiastical system, satisfying the bishops. The emphasis that the monks put on work and stability made a positive contribution to a culture that seemed to be spiraling downward, and, as we shall see, was especially favored by later kings (De Montclos 1988:27).

The Benedictine Rule became so popular in France that about 125 years after his death, the relics (bones) of St. Benedict were stolen from Monte Cassino by a monk and brought to a monastery in France (Fleury, today known as Saint-Benoît-sur-Loire). This became an important pilgrimage site and contributed to his popularity in France (Rey 1987:1586-87).

A third influence on Gallic monasticism, which also came from Italy, was due to Flavius Magnus Aurelius Cassiodorus (*Cassiodore*), a Roman scholar and statesman who became a monk. In the middle of the sixth century, he founded two monasteries, one of which was established to be a center for learning and culture. He created a large library of both classical and Christian books and sought to preserve the culture by the transcription of these works. He himself wrote significant works and encouraged others to do so (Latourette 1975:332).

Cassiodorus thus set the precedent for monasteries acting as academic centers. Since monasteries had always attracted some of the brightest and most intelligent members of society, this model was readily reproduced elsewhere (Latourette 1975:332).

Although monasteries in Gaul had always put some emphasis on learning, around 680 a significant wave of uniquely Christian schools opened up in Gaul within the monasteries. The rich could send their children and teenagers to these schools to learn how to read and write. Unlike in Italy, these schools only studied Christian texts. Similarly, more and more schools were started within the monasteries for the training of priests (De Montclos 1988:28).

Developing Problems within the Monasteries

The monasteries were the spiritual centers of Merovingian times, filled with many men (and an increasing number of women in the convents) who sought to love and serve the Lord with all their heart. However, a growing number of problems began to surface in these institutions.

The reasons that people had for entering a monastery were varied. At one end of the spectrum were those who entered out of a love for Christ. At the other end of the spectrum were those who were sent as political prisoners or because of family pressure. The net result was that monasteries sometimes became communities where Christian love must have seemed like a very distant goal.

A major problem that faced the abbots (*les abbés*) concerned the discipline and control of the monks under his authority. Describing one godly abbot, Gregory of Tours said, "He had one weakness, that he sought to rule the monks under his care not by commands but by entreaty" (591:227). But the abbot then had a vision of a river of fire with a bridge passing over it. "From this bridge will be hurled headlong anyone who is discovered to have been lacking in authority over those committed to his charge," (591:228) was the meaning of the vision. "From then on he was more severe with his monks" (591:228).

Violence seems to have been a way of life in the monasteries. Gregory tells another story of what happened once in Bordeaux. A novice was assigned to watch over some grain drying in the sun. Suddenly it looked like a thunderstorm would drench it, but he knew he did not have enough time to bring it into the barn. So he fell to his knees praying for God's protection of the grain. The abbot and other monks ran out to help save the grain. The abbot recognized what the monk in charge of the corn was doing, so he too fell down in prayer, and the corn was saved from rain and water damage. "He then told the youth to get up and ordered him to be seized and beaten. 'It is for you, my son,' said he, 'to grow more and more humble in the fear and service of God, not to puff yourself up with prodigies and miracles" (591:229). The abbot then had the young man locked up in his cell for a week to reflect on his sinfulness so that he would not become arrogant.

The perceived need for discipline in the monasteries continued to develop. One of the reasons that the Benedictine Rule functioned so well was that it required obedience to the abbot that was as important as obedience to Christ.

> The first degree of humility is obedience without delay. This becometh those who, on account of the holy subjection which they have promised, or of the fear of hell, or the glory of life everlasting, hold nothing dearer than Christ. As soon as anything hath been commanded by the Superior they permit no delay in the execution, as if the matter had been commanded by God Himself. Of these the Lord saith: "At the hearing of the ear he hath obeyed Me" (Ps 17[18]:45). And again He saith to the teachers: "He that heareth you heareth Me" (Lk 10:16) (Benedict of Nursia 540:Rule 5).

This, of course, caused major problems when one's abbot was not an especially godly man, as was too often the case when the rich and powerful controlled the abbeys. Another weakness of this system was that it put the word of a man on equal footing with the Word of God, a problem compounded by the fact that feeble human nature tends to be attracted to the visible, not the invisible, when the two are believed to have equal value.

Another problem that the monasteries faced was the question of control. Normally, the abbot, under the authority of Christ (and perhaps the pope, as was the case for the Benedictine monasteries) were responsible for the spiritual and material well-being of the communities, which included managing all the monastery owned (De Montclos 1988:28).

As time went on, many monasteries became quite rich. Often, a rich property owner would leave some or all of his property to a monastery after his death. Kings and queens, to please God or win favor with the bishops, would also sometimes give land to the monasteries (Gregory of Tours 591:182).

In the midst of a period of social chaos, the monasteries also became economic centers linked by a system of roadways. They were one of the few stable aspects of society. Because of this, they were coveted by those seeking power. Often the protectors, those who made donations or had military power, demanded the right to name the abbot, someone who would look after the protector's interests, rather than God's. This was a sure formula for spiritual decline (De Montclos 1988:28).

Another problem within the monasteries resulted from the fact that monastic life offered an alternative, and in many ways more attractive, way of life. People could choose a monastic life style because of its attractiveness, not because of their love for Christ. The order and discipline in the monastic culture was a welcomed alternative to the confusion, violence, sensuality, and decay which characterized everyday life outside the cloister. As mentioned before, obedience to the abbot tended to become as important as obedience to Christ. Likewise, poverty started to become an end in itself. The idea of giving up all one's possessions forever became a rule, rather than a tool to enable certain people to better serve Christ (Latourette 1975:334-36).

Another evangelical option which became a rule was celibacy. Certainly for those who possessed the gift, this lifestyle provided a means of better serving Christ. But for the vast majority of Christians who wanted to live fully for Christ, it must have been a horrible hurdle put on the narrow path of serving him. Even if someone converted (decided to become a monk) when he or she was already married, he or she would be expected to finish his or her life in sexual abstinence. Gregory of Tours tells the following story about a bishop at Clermont-Ferrand:

> He was a married man and, according to the custom of the church, his wife lived as a religious, apart from her husband. They both devoted themselves to prayer, charity and good works. As they were pursuing the even tenor of their lives, the woman was filled with the Devil's own malice, which is always hostile to holiness: for he inflamed her with desire for her husband and turned her into a second Eve. The Bishop's wife burned so hot with passion, and was overwhelmed by dark thoughts of a sinful nature, that she made her way through the pitch-black night to the church-house. When she found that everything was shut up for the night, she started to beat on the doors of the church-house and shout something like the following: 'Bishop! How long do you intend to remain asleep? How long do you propose to refuse to open these closed doors? Why do you scorn your lawful wife? Why do you shut your ears and refuse to listen to the words of Paul, who wrote: "Come together again, that Satan tempt you not." I am here! I am returning to you, not as to a stranger, but to one who belongs to me.' For a long time she went on shouting these things and others like them. In the end the Bishop forgot his religious scruples and ordered her to be admitted to his bedroom, where he had intercourse with her and then said that it was time for her to go. Later on he recovered his wits, and grieved for the sin which he had committed. He went off to a monastery in his diocese, with the intention of doing penance. With

lamentation and tears he atoned for his misdeeds, and finally came back to his own town (591:93-34).

Because of an over-emphasis placed on chastity, any sexual expression, even in marriage became classified as sin. Stories like this undoubtedly confused the common person on what it meant to be holy and live for Christ, and it must have scared many away from a monastic life, even though they might have truly wanted to serve Christ. Asceticism was replacing submission to Christ.

Missiological Applications

Though the Merovingian centuries seem far away and irrelevant to most people, an evangelical missionary can see in them the origin of many of the ideas he or she must battle against. The missionary can also gain some insights into French culture that can make him or her more effective in ministry, as well as learn from the examples of the Christians of this time.

Christian Wives and Their Non-Christian Husbands

Just as Clotilda found herself married to a non-Christian Clovis, so many women in the French evangelical churches have non-believing husbands. This is an impediment to growth for many of the women, but also an opportunity for ministry that should not be missed.

There are several reasons that there are so many Christian women with non-Christian husbands. Firstly, it seems that women are more open to the Gospel. They tend to be more open to relationships so this brings them more into contact with Christians and gives them more of a chance to hear the Gospel. Another reason is that men tend to feel the need to be macho (*le machisme*), and passively going to church does not respond to this need.

To respond to this situation, special efforts need to be made to reach men. "Sitting around and talking" activities might not be as effective as activities oriented around sports or accomplishing a well defined project. If men (apart from professional Christian workers) play a major role in directing the activities of the church and are the ones who are up front the most (but not uniquely, lest the women feel excluded), this communicates that there is a real place for men in church. Another way to show men that they have a place in the church is to involve them in service projects very early in their participation, perhaps even before their conversion in order to show them they have an important role to play.

Since women are in the majority in most evangelical churches, they also have special ministry needs. Women's groups are relatively easy to put in place and meet a real need if the right people are leading and teaching them. There needs to be teaching on how to live with and witness to non-believing husbands.

Another concern deals with young women (and men) who are not yet married. So many of the older women have non-believing husbands that marriage with a non-believer could be considered normal and acceptable. Teaching on the need to form Christian families and how they should function needs to occur regularly, but with much love and gentleness so as not to discourage or needlessly offend those who have already made bad choices concerning a spouse.

Helping the Poor

Just as the bishops defended the interests of the common person during the time of the barbarian invasions, the modern Catholic Church sets a very high priority on helping the poor and homeless. This is the role that the average French person expects the Church to play, and gives value and meaning to being Catholic. For example, in the early twenty-first century, the only orthodox Catholic personality to have a high positive response in public opinion polls is Abbé Pierre, an elderly man who is the national voice for the poor and homeless. Another example is found in the large Catholic church built near Paris in Bussy-St.-Georges in 1998. Of the ten or so rooms in the complex, two of them were for housing transient homeless people, but none specifically for catechism or youth ministry.

As a religious leader, it will be assumed that the missionary will be a defender of the rights of the poor. This gives the missionary a positive image in the community, but at the same time it implies that we really are expected to be helping the poor.

Each missionary needs to find the correct balance between social work, evangelism, and church development. This balance may be harder for him or her to find in the French culture because most cross-cultural missionaries come from rural or suburban areas where they may have had little or no interaction with the poor on a regular basis. But in France this is not the case. Most new churches are created with a majority of people that have a less than average salary. The poor are far more open to the Gospel than the rich are, and they seem to have a greater fascination with America than the rich do because of what they see on television. All of this means that the North American missionary will probably be dealing with the poor much more in France than he or she did before.

The missionary needs to be aware that working with the poor is quite stressful. They can have very dependent personalities and their needs are quite visible. It can be quite discouraging when one becomes close to someone and invests a lot of time and effort into his or her life, and then the person reverts back to that same self-destructive behavior that originally led to the poverty. Under the direction of God's Spirit, each missionary must discern how to divide his or her time between those who are poor and needy and those who have a more stable lifestyle.

The Concept of Cultural Level

In the modern Anglo-Saxon world, the idea that one culture is superior to another would not generally be considered an acceptable point of view. But this is not the case in France. The difference between Gaul under the Romans and Gaul under the barbarians is undeniable. The cultures that value literacy and creativity over war and violence are still considered superior by the majority of the French.

Another difference between French and Anglo-Saxon thinking is that the French think of culture as belonging not just to a nation or a people, but also as something that can be quantitatively possessed by individuals. The French readily speak of one's *niveau culturel* (cultural level), meaning how one has been raised and trained, including both the formal, informal, and non-formal education the person has received. One of the main duties of the government is to help raise the *niveau culturel* of the children of immigrants through education, so that they will be able to be as intelligent, responsible, analytic, creative, and quick thinking as the average French person, enabling them to fully integrate into society.

In any context in France, it is difficult to blend people of different *niveaux culturels*. People tend to feel most comfortable with people who are most like themselves. This is true in America as well. People tend to go to universities or live in neighborhoods that are filled with people with the same *niveau culturel* as themselves. But in France, the government has had a policy for generations that cities must avoid social segregation so that no large area becomes a ghetto composed entirely of poor people or people of one ethnic group. This means, for example, that everyone who lives in a city or the suburbs also lives within walking distance of government financed housing projects for the poor. The urban and suburban French, although segregated socially, are always geographically close to those of other economic classes. Thus all churches will have contact with people of various *niveaux culturels*, but when a significant portion of the church consists of people with a low *niveau culturel*, it is difficult to attract anyone else.

Another phenomenon is that in a given organization, the *niveau culturel* of the people attracted to the organization will in general be lower than that of the leaders of the organization. People want to have leaders that are capable of truly leading them. This means that missionaries are likely to start a church only with people who have a cultural level lower than theirs, apart from the grace of God. So a missionary preparing for ministry in France needs to make sure he or she is educated as much as possible in the things dear to the French mind (art, literature, science, history, economics, and sociology, for example) in order to be capable of reaching the greatest number of people. Likewise, it is important to seek to develop leadership that has an elevated *niveau culturel* so that they, too, can reach a maximum number of people. This, of course, is about ten million times easier to say than to do.

The Irrelevance of Salvation

Two elements of medieval theology that developed during this period have had an enormous impact on how the French view salvation. When the Council of Orange attempted to define and integrate the doctrine of baptismal regeneration and predestination, it basically said to the common person that salvation is something very complex and difficult to understand. Ever since, it has not been clear who would be saved, and this perpetual ambiguity has resulted in a general indifference.

Furthermore, the idea that infant baptism puts a child in a spiritual state superior to a child who has not received it makes God seem unjust and arbitrary. Many people do not want to have anything to do with this sort of god.

The doctrine of purgatory has also made the question of salvation seem irrelevant because it means that even the most wicked Catholic will probably eventually get to heaven. The idea of saying masses and praying for the dead to reduce their punishment does not fit into a Cartesian mindset, so this also makes God seem unjust and arbitrary. Thus, to many French people, the idea of an afterlife seems incomprehensible at best, confused, worthless, and illogical at worst.

For this reason, missionaries and other evangelists need to emphasize the present benefits of eternal life. The benefits that come after this life do not interest the average person. Like Israel in the Old Testament, what interests them is that which affects their present life, the here and now. The good news that they can have a life filled with love, joy, and peace is more relevant to their felt needs than the fact that they can live forever and escape eternal destruction.

Roman Protection from Ungodly Leaders

The Gallic church accepted the authority of pope Gregory the Great in order to help prevent further decay within the church. Similarly, even today there is still the idea that the pope is a source of moral stability that helps counteract what modern ungodly leaders would do to the country. Thus the Catholic Church still has a certain respect by approximately half of the population, principally those who consider themselves Catholic. Although almost everyone would say they disagree with the pope on certain questions, (especially concerning birth control and condoms, two independent questions in many people's minds), they still have a certain respect for him and his visit to the country is an important event.

Confusion Concerning Sin and Sexuality

Since the beginning of the Middle Ages, there has been confusion in France between sexuality in general and sexual immorality. The Christians of this epoch began to believe that to be a true believer, one had to live in abstinence. Ever since, those who have chosen to live totally committed to God (priests, monks, and nuns) have had to choose a life of celibacy. Although it has long been taught in the Catholic Church that marriage is good, this truth is not modeled by Catholic leadership, and the message that many people have received is that all sex is sin. In the popular mind, the original sin (*le péché originel*) that was committed by Adam and Eve was that of having a sexual relationship.

The natural conclusion that one draws from this belief is that Christianity certainly is not for "real men" and it really is not too appropriate for even a minimally vivacious woman either. This might be another partial explanation of why both

Protestant and Catholic churches usually have many more women than men attending. This situation calls for several responses by the evangelical missionary. First of all, he or she should model a healthy sexuality. Most French have never seen a marriage modeled by a Christian leader. The missionary couple needs to model in their marriage what it means for Christ to love the church and for the church to respond to Christ (Eph. 5:22-33). The missionary also needs to teach the Biblical view of sexuality. Since the Evangelical view of birth control and sexuality for non-procreative reasons are different from the Roman Catholic stance on these issues, the missionary needs to make a special effort to present a biblical theology on such topics. The idea that sex within marriage, even without a procreative goal, is a gift from God for expressing a couple's intimacy can be very attractive to those considering Evangelical Christianity

5
The Church under the Carolingians: The Eighth through Tenth Centuries

From a North American perspective, the second half of the first millennium is often assumed to be a fairly uniform period, void of any human progress whatsoever. Most North Americans would find it difficult to cite any important achievements that occurred during the period between the Fall of Rome in the fifth century and the end of the tenth century when cities and trade began to develop once again. However, the European point of view is quite different. Certainly, this epoch contains some of the darkest periods of Western history, but it also contains a glimmer of hope which foreshadows the European dominance of the second millennium. In between the wars and reigns of the Merovingians (the fifth through seventh centuries) and the cultural decay during the reigns of the latter Carolingians (end of the ninth through the tenth centuries), one finds a period of remarkable European glory, the Empire of Charlemagne and its accompanying academic renaissance (Rey 1987:376-77).

Charlemagne's Europe has ever since been the model of unity sought by Europe's leaders. Louis XIV, Napoleon, and Hitler all dreamed of a unified Europe. Even today, the European Community (the former Common Market) is in some ways trying to recreate Charlemagne's unified Europe (Rey 1987:376-77).

The Early Carolingians

Arnulf, Bishop of Metz in the early seventh century, was the first prominent member of a family that gradually became more and more powerful in Gaul. He was also the head of the ancestral line of kings and emperors who would be known as the Carolingians. For the first time, the power in France was coming into the hands of a family for whom Christianity was part of their fundamental identity (Rey 1987:106).

The Decline of the Merovingians

Upon the death of a Merovingian king, his lands would be divided among his sons. This was a constant encouragement for the heirs to war against one another. Several times, the Frankish Kingdom was united under one king, but most of the time, it was under the control of several competing kings. Various individuals found ways to profit from the wars, and several managed to become richer and more powerful than the kings who continued to hold the royal title. The most powerful person in the kingdom would take the position known as the Mayor of the Palace, and it was he who would direct the kingdom and the puppet king. The actual kings (*les rois fainéants,* the idle kings) were kept in submission by allowing them to live in a state of complete debauchery, where they had only pleasures and readily gave all responsibilities to the Mayor of the Palace. By the beginning of the eighth century the Frankish Kingdom was united under the authority of one of the descendents of Arnulf, Pepin of Herstal, Mayor of the Palace (Frémy and Frémy 1998:603-04).

Charles Martel and the Muslim Invasions

In 714, Pepin's son Charles inherited the title Mayor of the Palace. Because of his organizational and military genius, he was able to keep the kingdom intact. His use of force earned him the title "Martel" which means hammer (Rey 1987:379).

In 732 Charles achieved his greatest military victory, eternally meriting a prestigious place in history; he definitively defeated the Muslim invaders coming up from Spain at the Battle of Poitiers. For a century, Islam had been advancing, across Africa and then up through Spain. Given the general reign of decline in the Frankish Kingdom, it must have looked like simply a matter of time before the Franks would also fall to the Muslims. However, Charles Martel was able to stop them. After this victory, his prestige was so great that when the last of the Merovingian kings, Thierry III, died, Charles felt secure enough in his position to not appoint a new king, though he did not dare appoint himself king (Rivière 1986:26-27).

During this time, things were evolving in Rome so that the papacy would have to look to the West for help rather than the East, where the remains of the original Roman Empire were still more or less intact. In the fourth decade of the eighth century, there was a great conflict between the pope, Gregory III, and the emperor, Leo III. The emperor was against the use of icons in worship, while the pope was for their use. The pope excommunicated the emperor, and all relations between the Roman church and the Byzantine Empire were over. The pope tried to turn to Charles Martel for help (for protection against the Lombard threat), but both Charles and the pope died in 741 (Latourette 1975:354).

Pepin the Short and Christendom

Upon the death of Charles Martel, his son Pepin the Short (*Pépin le Bref*) inherited the kingdom. He was to become the first King of the Franks to have a undeniably positive relationship with the church (Rey 1987:1390).

In the early years of Pepin's reign, he regained territory that had been long lost to the Muslims and was able to stamp out interior revolts. Because there was still one Merovingian laying claim to the Kingdom of the Franks, Pepin sent a message asking the new pope who should be king, the one who has the power (the Mayor of the Palace) or the one who does not have it (the Merovingian). By making this request of the pope, Pepin was giving tacit assent to the principle that the pope had the authority both to establish and depose kings (Rivière 1986:27).

The pope, facing the growing menace of the Lombards, decided to grant Pepin his request and had him crowned King of the Franks by Boniface, an English missionary who had full papal support. Several years later, the pope met Pepin at St. Denis, near Paris and personally crowned him King of the Franks. For the first time, the temporal and spiritual powers were completely intertwined for the Franks; obedience to the king was obedience to the church (Latourette 1975:354).

To thank the pope, Pepin sent troupes to Italy to ward off the encroaching Lombards. Pepin gave the recovered territories to the pope, thus establishing the Papal States, confusing even further the distinction between temporal and spiritual powers in the Roman Church. At this time the notion of Christendom began to develop, the idea that some states were Christian and shared a common culture which united them against those states outside of Christendom (Rivière 1986:27).

The English Missionaries and the Development of Parishes

In the latter part of the seventh century, English missionaries started to come to the continent to evangelize the pagan rural population, just as the Irish missionaries had done so before. The first important figure was Willibrord, who was one of the first evangelists to bring the Gospel to the parts of the continent north of the borders of the former Roman Empire. Although he worked primarily outside of what is now France (in Friesland, roughly equivalent to the modern Netherlands north of the Maas River), his influence was keenly felt throughout the Frankish Kingdom. Willibrord sought and received papal support. He also sought and received support from the Mayors of the Palace. Thus his evangelization had both a spiritual and political impact; to become Christian implied either submission to the Franks or at least some sort of acceptance of Frankish expansion (Latourette 1975:347-48).

One of Willibrord's disciples, Winfrith, also known by his Latin name Boniface, played an important role in the evangelization of what is now known as Germany. His fame grew and in the middle of the eighth century, the pope called on him to reform the entire Frankish church. For many years, the Merovingian kings had taken bishoprics, abbeys, and churches and distributed them to whomever they chose. This, of course, led to corruption on virtually every level of ecclesiastical life. With the backing of the pope and with Pepin, Boniface traveled from region to region, reorganizing the church by strengthening the authority of Rome over the bishops and by reestablishing the authority of the bishops over the churches and abbeys (Latourette 1975:348-49).

This resulted in the gradual establishment of parishes, the idea that a number of churches were under the authority of a bishop, and that the territory under a bishop was divided up into sectors (parishes), each one having their own church. Most of the private churches were brought under the authority of the bishop. The parish church (which became the heart of the village) was the place to which all had to come for the sacraments and to pay the mandatory *dîme* (tithe), a variable fraction of each family's harvest. Although the strengthening of the ecclesiastical structure was instituted to reform the church, the new structure created an even greater temptation for the worldly powers of the newly developing feudal system to seek to control it (De Montclos 1988:26-29).

Charlemagne

Upon Pepin's death in 768, the kingdom was divided among his two sons. Several years later, one of the sons died, and the remaining Charles (later to be known as Charles the Great, or *Charlemagne*) gained control of the entire kingdom. He was a military genius and brought most of Western and Central Europe under his control, creating the largest contiguous European empire since the Roman Empire, a feat which has never since been equaled (Rey 1987:376-77).

The Church under the Carolingians

To govern this vast empire, Charlemagne put in place a system of government which would define the feudal system in the centuries that followed. The capital of the empire was at Aix-la-Chapelle which became its academic and administrative center. The empire was divided among 700 counts who were chosen by Charlemagne and held their position until their death or until Charlemagne replaced them for political reasons. In what remained of the cities, the bishops, who continued to be named by the king, remained the principal leaders, both spiritually and, perhaps even more so, politically (Rivière 1986:29-30).

Another distinctive of Charlemagne and his work was that he was the first king who appeared to sincerely be concerned about pleasing God and doing good to the church (Latourette 1975:355). Several, but probably not the majority, of the kings who would follow would also have this concern.

Reforms in the Church

Charlemagne continued the Frankish custom of giving bishoprics and abbeys to his friends. However, he generally tried to choose godly and educated men to fill these posts (Latourette 1975:355-56).

Charlemagne put an end to private churches where the priest was chosen by the local lord. He brought all the priests in a given geographical area under the authority of the appropriate bishop (De Montclos 1988:26).

Charlemagne also restructured and enlarged the system of archbishops. The archbishops were to have authority over a group of bishops, thus ensuring greater ecclesiastical unity. It also provided a structure for Charlemagne to have more control over the bishops. Through this new structure, priests were directed to teach a minimum to their parishioners (The Lord's Prayer, the Apostles' Creed, and the Ten

Commandments) and to use a common liturgy developed by Rome. This liturgy was in Latin, the language of the educated, so although it assured unity and conformity in the church, it was incomprehensible to the common person (De Montclos 1988:29-30).

Charlemagne also strengthened the church by enforcing the tithe. In principal, every family was to give ten percent (but the actual figure varied quite a bit) of his harvest to the local priest (Latourette 1975:356).

Pope Leon III crowned Charlemagne emperor on Christmas Day 800. He thus created a new sort of Christian Roman Empire where the temporal and spiritual were completely intertwined (Rivière 1986:29).

Charlemagne's Personal Piety

A major part of Charlemagne's legacy was his personal piety. As a sort of Founding Father of France, he has served as a model over the centuries of what it means to be good. His loyalty to friends, his faithfulness to his children (but not especially to his ten wives and concubines), his desire to do good to those around him, his openness to strangers and foreigners (*les étrangers*), and his moderation in food and drink served to define what it meant for a person to be a good Christian (Latourette 1975:355).

> He was firm and steady in his human relationships, developing friendship easily, keeping it up with care and doing everything he possibly could for anyone whom he had admitted this degree of intimacy.
>
> He paid such attention to the upbringing of his sons and daughters that he never sat down to table without them when he was at home, and never set out on a journey without taking them with him. . . .

> Throughout . . . his life he so won the love and favor of all his fellow human beings, both at home and abroad, that no one ever leveled against him the slightest charge of cruelty or injustice.
>
> He loved foreigners and took great pains to make them welcome. . . . He considered that his reputation for hospitality and the advantage of the good name which he acquired more than compensated for the great nuisance of their being there. . . .
>
> He was moderate in his eating and drinking, and especially so in drinking; for he hated to see drunkenness in any man, and even more so in himself and his friends (Einhard c. 833:75-78).

Although Charlemagne's biographer undoubtedly exaggerates concerning some aspects of his reputation, this passage underlines the qualities that helped establish Charlemagne's renown.

The Carolingian Renaissance

One of the most marked changes of this period was the revival of the written word. For hundreds of years, writing had been in decline. Charlemagne tried to stop this trend by establishing a palace school in Aix-la-Chapelle. The school played an important part in the empire and was one of Charlemagne's favorite institutions. Its most famous instructor was the Anglo-Saxon Alcuin, who was also one of Charlemagne's closest advisors. Alcuin wrote commentaries on the Bible, theological treatises, and established other schools in monasteries throughout the Empire, seeking to raise the educational level of monks. He developed a new system of writing with minuscules and majuscules, which essentially is the same system we use today (Latourette 1975:357).

One of the most important works carried on in the Carolingian schools was that of copying manuscripts, both sacred and profane. If it had not been for the work of these schools, the vast majority of texts from the Roman Empire would not have been passed on to us. By uniting classical and Christian learning, the Carolingian schools created a new culture which would dominate the occidental world for the next millennium (De Montclos 1988:32-33).

Christian Expansion

With the reestablishment of the Empire, and the development of a fundamentally new culture, the expansion of Christianity took on new forms under Charlemagne. Military conquest and evangelism merged together, the one becoming indistinguishable from the other (Latourette 1975:350).

The general pattern of Christian expansion consisted of an initial military invasion followed by missionary work which introduced Carolingian culture. This would be followed by revolts, a second military defeat, resulting finally in a gradual acceptance of the new culture. When a people group was defeated, the terms of peace generally included conversion to the Catholic faith. So the revolts that followed were often accompanied by outbreaks of pagan religions, which the missionaries would try to squelch, occasionally becoming martyrs in the process. Those who refused to be baptized or who continued pagan practices were sometimes put to death (Neill 1986:67-69).

This was the first time that force was used to such a degree to bring about conversions to Christianity. Although some monks, such as Alcuin, opposed the use of force for converting peoples, others found it compatible with the Christian faith. The Council of Orange in the sixth century, which had papal approval, clearly taught that baptism gave grace to all who received it, enabling them to perform what was necessary for salvation. So by forcing groups to be baptized (which meant becoming Christian), Charlemagne believed that he was helping them come closer to salvation (Latourette 1975:351-52).

Military conquest thus became a sort of evangelism. The natural result of this type of evangelism was a shallow, but enduring, form of Christianity that concentrated on outward ceremonies but had little impact on an individual's life. Nevertheless, wherever Christianity was forced on a people, monasteries arose for those who wanted to follow Christ in a more sincere way (Neill 1986:66-69).

Imposition of the Benedictine Rule

Another innovation that Charlemagne introduced to the Gallic church was the mandatory use of the Benedictine Rule in the monasteries. Up to this point, many monasteries acted more or less independently of each other or of the church. Under Charlemagne, a uniform code was imposed on them, thus bringing them under the authority of both the emperor and the pope. The structure that the Benedictine Rule imposed continued to be a source of economic and social stability, but with the impetus that came from Charlemagne's support, the monasteries also became the principal centers of learning and culture in France (Rivière 1986:31-32).

This resulted in greater conformity and less spiritual creativity. By enforcing culturally determined rules in all the monasteries, these institutions, like all aspects of Carolingian civilization, tended to lose the distinction between what was distinctly Christian and what was not. More often than ever before, they came under the control of unscrupulous abbots who had little concern for the things of God (De Montclos 1988:30).

The Carolingian Decline

When Charlemagne died in 814, his only living son Lewis the Pious (*Louis le Pieux*) inherited the whole empire. Because of his Christian principles, Lewis refused to use force to extract money from his nobles and the lands owned by the Church, resulting in a loss of imperial power. Even before Lewis' death, the empire was suffering from the infighting of Lewis' sons, each one seeking to overpower the others (Rivière 1986:32).

At Lewis' death in 840, the empire was in a state of civil war. In 843, the three remaining brothers made peace and divided the empire in three parts, creating a Europe roughly equivalent to what we know today. Between the country of the West (France) and the country of the East (Germany), was a middle country approximately corresponding to the modern Netherlands, Belgium, Luxembourg, Switzerland and Italy (Rivière 1986:33).

Soon after the peace treaty, the king of France, Charles the Bald (*Charles le Chauve*) resumed fighting to regain the empire and he was eventually crowned emperor in 873. However, his actual power was limited. To gain his title, Charles had to give away almost all his land, thus making him and his successors too weak to have a real influence over those who were supposed to be his subjects (Rivière 1986:34).

By the end of the tenth century, the territories truly under the authority of the king were limited to a small area north of Paris. The most powerful man in the country was Hugh Capet (*Hugues Capet*), his surname referring to the half of the cloak of St. Martin, the most precious relic in France, which his family possessed. Upon the death of the last Carolingian, Louis V, in 987, the various lords and bishops of France elected Hugh Capet to be the new king, the head of the *Capétien* dynasty (Rivière 1986:34-35).

The Viking Invasions and the Rise of Feudalism

Early in the ninth century, Charlemagne's territorial expansion towards the north had been stopped by the Scandinavians in Denmark. A very strong tension existed between these two European powers for a generation, and by 850 the invading Scandinavians known as Vikings were regularly ravishing the north and west of France. These invasions, added to the general political decline of the Empire, resulted in a major economic slowdown of the country and a general cultural regression (Rivière 1986:34).

In addition, Saracen (Arab, *les Sarassins*) invaders from the south and Hungarian invaders from the east wreaked havoc in the south and east of France. The king of France had little power to do anything and the country fell into general chaos. In 877 the king Charles the Bald gave up the right to name counts and made the title a hereditary right, effectively making the counts local kings who would battle continually among themselves for power. Vassals would swear allegiance to their superiors, providing them with military service in order to have the use of land. On the bottom of this social pyramid were the serfs who were little more than poorly treated slaves. This golden age of feudalism was perhaps the darkest of what North Americans call the Dark Ages. Cities virtually died out, and trade and the use of money almost ceased. The bishoprics and abbeys became simple fiefs in the hands of feudal lords, who often had no Christian values at all (Rivière 1986:34).

In 896, some Vikings established a permanent settlement near the mouth of the Seine River from which they based their raids. Fifteen years later, in order to prevent further destruction of the country, the king Charles the Simple (*Charles le Simple*) offered them permanent control of Normandy (*la Normandie,* the Land of the Norse Men) if they would become Christian and accept, at least in principle, to become vassals of the king. Under the leadership of Rollo (*Rollon*), the Vikings accepted this offer and within a generation the Viking invasions had come to an end, though the interior battles between feuding lords continued (Frémy and Frémy 1998:605).

Increased Papal Authority

As in the time of Gregory the Great, anarchy in France caused an element within the church to turn to Rome for stability. In a period where the temporal and spiritual powers were completely intertwined, corruption developed within the church as never before. Two practices that became more and more common were *le nicolaïsme* (priests living with concubines) and simony (selling relics, bishoprics, dioceses, sacraments or anything else that could bring a price). Those who were in the church for spiritual reasons began, more than ever, to call for the spiritual authority to be above the temporal authority (De Montclos 1988:31-35).

The spirit of the age is very dramatically portrayed in a series of documents produced in France around 850 known as the *Decretals of Pseudo-Isadore* or the *False Decretals*. This collection of documents contained the canons of the fifty four Councils, a treatise on the primitive church, and a collection of true and apocryphal letters supposedly written by the popes beginning with Clement in the first century. The popes of the first three centuries are quoted as saying things which were actually written in the fourth through sixth centuries, and the popes of the next three centuries state things written in the seventh through ninth centuries. This gave authority to the ecclesiology and theology of the early Middle Ages (Latourette 1975:342).

Included in these documents was what was known as the *Donation of Constantine*, a spurious decree by Constantine which stated that he had given the pope authority over the secular state, emphasizing the superiority of the spiritual over the temporal. Other keys ideas found in the *Decretals* include papal supremacy over the church and the independence of bishops from secular authorities and laws (Latourette 1975:342).

The *Decretals* gave historical justification to a papal-centric church. This was an encouragement to the bishops of France who were seeking to preserve the little influence and independence that they had. During the second half of the ninth century the documents circulated widely throughout Western Europe, accepted everywhere as authentic. The pope Nicholas I, pope 858 to 867, known as the Great, declared that the *Decretals* were truly contained in the Roman archives, thereby reinforcing his authority over the Western Church and Western Civilization (Douglas 1978:708, Saltet 1909:11).

The teachings of the *Decretals* became foundational to later medieval theology and were maintained by Rome to be true up through the Counter Reformation, although they had been shown to be forgeries by various scholars beginning in the fifteenth century. The doctrine of papal supremacy continues to have a major influence on the Catholic Church today, though perhaps not as much as some Evangelicals claim (Douglas 1978:368).

Monastic Renewal at Cluny

One bright spot in this very dark period of history concerned the monastery in Cluny, located north of Lyon. The only way that monasteries of this epoch could escape being controlled or sold by feudal chieftains was to obtain a charter that put the monastery directly under the authority of Rome and remain large and organized enough to resist those who would try to secularize it. No other monastery was more successful in doing this than Cluny (De Montclos 1988:35-36).

In 909, William the Pious (*Guillaume le Pieux*) of Aquitaine granted a charter to the monastery which assured that it did not have to obey either feudal lords or bishops, but was directly under the authority of the Pope. Thus Cluny's early abbots, who were godly men chosen from among the monastic community, were able to lead a spiritual community in the midst of the corruption of the age (Latourette 1975:417-18).

In spite of power-hungry princes and lords, violence and lawlessness, corruption and oppressed masses, the monastery of Cluny provided a place where order reigned, one could pray, and the fastidious liturgies foreshadowed the glory of the coming Kingdom. The popularity of the monastery was immense, and in the two hundred years which followed the founding of Cluny, about twelve hundred monasteries were founded or reformed by monks coming from Cluny, all of which were under Cluny's authority. The most famous of the monks of Cluny was Hildebrand, who became pope Gregory VII in 1073 and attempted to initiate major ecclesiastical reforms in the eleventh century (Rey 1987:42).

Missiological Applications

The end of the first millennium was a difficult epoch for the Church. However, there are several things worth noting for the North American evangelical missionary.

Carolingian Piety

Charlemagne was known as an expert in human relations, a model father (though not a model husband), the most faithful of friends, a welcomer of foreigners, and a model of moderation. These qualities have become the standard qualities that are expected of French leaders. American missionaries might expect to be accepted as leaders because of their commitment, expertise and efficiency, values that hold a high position in American churches. They might not see themselves as "people persons," or they might never have experienced an intimate friendship with someone (from a French perspective, Americans are often seen as being quite shallow). In many North American evangelical circles, the ability to welcome foreigners is not of great importance. Likewise, moderation in eating is not a strong point for many North American Christians. However, if they are missing these Carolingian qualities it will be hard for the French to accept their leadership.

If a missionary is significantly overweight, he or she will be seen as a glutton, lacking self-control. If he or she is perceived as being more concerned about efficiency in time management than about individuals, he or she will be perceived as being unloving. If the missionary is not open to foreigners, he or she will be considered racist, the ultimate in French political incorrectness (even among those who are quite racist). If the missionary does not take care of his or her family, he or she will be considered worse than an unbeliever. Certainly, some of these qualities that Charlemagne modeled have a certain biblical ring to them, and North American missionaries coming to France will especially need to master them if they want to be effective leaders.

The Concept of Europe

Charlemagne's Empire, even more so than the Roman Empire, covers essentially the same territory today as the European Community (formerly known as the Common Market). The European ideal of living in peace and prosperity with one's neighbors in a common system closed to outsiders is an ideal upheld by all the French except those of the extreme right and left. Whereas few Americans feel that a fundamental aspect to their identity is being a "North American," for more and more French, being "European" is essential to their cultural identity.

For the North American missionary, the transformation caused by the Europeanization of France can make church planting a little bit easier because the range of what is culturally acceptable is widening. If a church can appear to be European, it comes across as being somewhat culturally relevant to a larger audience than if it just appeared to be American (which is how all churches which begin with only American missionaries appear). So if the North Americans can work in partnership with other European missionaries (such as those from Northern Ireland, England, or Germany), their credibility will probably be enhanced, at least among those people who are sensitive to the value of a strong and stable European Community. Certainly, however, working in partnership with a French church planter would have the potential to enhance one's cultural relevancy even more.

The Remnants of Feudalism

The classical pyramidal structure of feudalism (with the king at the top and the mass of plebeians at the bottom) is still very much alive in France, though it is now multidimensional (economic, educational, and political). The church planting missionary in France will especially have to deal with the political pyramid which exists. In a very simplified form, the President is at the top, followed by the Prime Minister and then his or her ministers. Then come the Representatives (*les députés*) followed by the mayors of the 36,000 cities and towns (*communes*). Underneath the mayors are the local leaders of people grouped in clubs, churches and associations (*les présidents des associations*). On the bottom of the pyramid are the common people who are usually members of various *associations*.

The missionary who functions as a pastor will be in the level between mayors and the common people. This has two major applications, one concerning the mayor who is above him, and one concerning the people in the church led by the missionary.

The pastor's relationship with the mayor is of utmost importance. If the church wants to use a public building, or rent and use a private building, or have some type of public meeting, or obtain a building permit, it must have the mayor's approval. So the pastor must do all that is possible to have a good relationship with the mayor. If the mayor believes that it is politically advantageous for him or her to favor the church, he or she will do it. But if he or she feels it is politically advantageous to oppose the church, he or she will do that as well (this is the more common case). The pastor, as the main representative of the church, must do everything possible to convince the mayor that having an evangelical church in his or her town is a good thing. This can be done by having formal (but friendly) meetings with the mayor, providing information on Protestantism or on other evangelical churches in the region, or by participating in municipal activities. In general, the more visible and culturally relevant the church is, the better.

Likewise, the pastor-missionary will also be the authority directly above the common person in the church. This means that the pastor will have incredible opportunities to lead and influence those in the church, if the pastoral ministry is anchored in love and merits the respect of those to be led. The pastor will have great authority and most people will look to the pastor for guidance and direction. But similarly, the pastor will be the first one to be attacked when individuals are not happy. Rebellion and revolution are the inherent rights of those at the bottom of the pyramid, and they will not hesitate to use these methods if a pastor's leadership does not meet their needs or expectations. Therefore, a North American pastor-missionary can expect to have many opportunities to lead but also many painful experiences of opposition, depending on how the pastoral ministry is perceived by those in the church.

Similarly, the average person often sees himself as powerless to change things. He or she might be hesitant to bring up matters for discussion or incapable of proposing changes in a non-confrontational way. His or her tendency would be to assume that no one would listen to him or her because of his or her social position. So missionaries need to continually emphasize that everyone has the right to propose new ideas and discuss them together, since each Christian is an equally valuable member of the body of Christ.

The Church as a Refuge

Just as the Cluny monasteries flourished because they provided a place of refuge in a chaotic age, today's evangelical churches can do the same.

We can offer people a source of personal, psychological stability, a community where they feel loved and accepted, and an intellectual framework upon which they can build their lives. Currently, there is much bias against all forms of Christianity because the Catholic church has failed to provide these things for most French people for many centuries. So the challenge is not only to provide this sort of refuge, but also to expose people to it so that they can make an informed choice.

To expose people to the Gospel and the refuge that can be found in an evangelical church, there are three common approaches used by North American missionaries. The first could be called "confrontational evangelism." The missionary knocks on doors, speaks at open air meetings, conducts surveys with people on the street, or asks permission to do some sort of Gospel presentation with an individual. This type of evangelism usually asks for an immediate response and does not seem to be very effective in the current climate of mistrust and fear of cults. It was far more effective in the 1970s when ideological confrontations were in vogue and it was culturally acceptable to seek truth. Today, the idea of truth has been replaced with practicality and few believe that absolute truth exists. "Confrontational evangelism" works best today among youth, who are less hardened against Christianity and are more willing to experiment with different philosophies.

The second method of evangelism used by North American missionaries is "friendship evangelism," where the missionary slowly develops friendships with people around him or her, hoping that the person will gradually become interested in the Gospel as he or she sees the missionary live out its implications. This method has the advantage that the Gospel is communicated through a relationship rather than just through intellectual ideas. It helps a new Christian (or seeker) integrate into a church because he or she already has a solid relationship with someone in it. However, this method's effectiveness is quite limited because of the time demands required by developing and maintaining a friendship, especially in France where the idea of friendship is much more intimate than in North America. It would seem quite difficult for a missionary, even if he or she did nothing else, to have more than about ten true friendships deep enough to really share all of what is happening in his or her life. And if he or she would have that many true friendships, the missionary would have little time to work in a church or develop new relationships, and there is certainly no guarantee that any of these people would be interested in the Gospel, much less that they would eventually decide to follow Christ.

The third method of evangelism used by North American missionaries is what could be called "harvest evangelism." It presupposes that at any given moment God is already working in certain people's lives. Because of the Holy Spirit's work of convicting people of sin and its consequences, there are always certain people somewhere in a community who are open to the Gospel. They may not know that they are open to the Gospel, or that the Gospel even exists, but, being under the conviction of the Holy Spirit and in some way already seeking God, they are ready to start responding when given the opportunity.

To do this sort of evangelism, the missionary must do all he or she can to give these people the opportunity to start responding. Since there might be only a few of these people at

The Church under the Carolingians   113

any given time in a community of tens of thousands, it is extremely difficult to find them through personal contacts. Thus the missionary uses culturally relevant means of bringing a part of the Gospel message to as many of these thousands of people as he or she can through literature distribution, broadly advertised musical or drama presentations, a highly visible presence in the community, evangelistic campaigns with young people coming from outside the church, or by any other method which will offer hope and catch the eye of the person who is already seeking God. The person is given the opportunity to respond (by calling a phone number or by visiting a church or an outreach activity) and at this point the relationship with the missionary (or another Christian) begins. Little by little, the Christian can progressively explain the Gospel in a way that this person can understand, answering his or her questions as they come up, modeling Christ's love as the relationship progresses, and introducing the person to the church, Christ's body, the true refuge from all that caused the person to start seeking God.

The advantages of this type of evangelism are numerous. First of all, the missionary uses his time and energy with people who to some degree are already seeking God and are open to the Gospel. Secondly, it reflects the apostle Paul's model of going to those who are the most open. Thirdly, it leads people to the church who realize that they have needs and are thus more prone to spiritual change.

However, this method also has its drawbacks. It requires a certain cultural expertise in mass communications that not all missionaries possess in order to effectively bring the initial offer to the multitudes. Secondly, the culturally relevant methods of touching the masses are expensive (attractive church brochures, advertisements, concerts, and so on) and might be beyond the missionary's means. Thirdly, this type of evangelism can attract "problem people," people who have suffered greatly or are overwhelmed by the problems in their life, often bringing significant psychological baggage into their relationships.

"Harvest evangelism" requires lots of flexibility in the missionary's schedule because he or she will need to invest much time and effort into helping the one person in a thousand who responds when the opportunity arises (not a week or two later!). It also requires that the church offer a true refuge consisting of a relatively complete program of high quality activities which will meet the needs of all life-phase groups within the community of seekers and believers: Children, youth, students, singles, and marrieds. This is not an easy task when the church consists of only a handful of people. It is not easy, but it is possible by the grace of God!

6
The Church in the Second and Third Millenniums

The purpose of this book has been to discuss the religious history of France up to the year 1000, the part of French history which is the most obscure for most North American missionaries. Certainly, the last one thousand years of religious history in France has had an equally great (or greater) impact on the current spiritual situation of the country. However, an in depth examination of this period is beyond the scope of this study. This final chapter contains a brief overview of the major events and movements of the period 1000-2000. It concludes with several trends, rather than missiological applications, which, I believe, will have a great impact on missions work in the third millennium.

The Church in the Second Millennium

The last thousand years of religious history in France are even more rich and complex than those of the first millennium. This overview will simply highlight some of the major events and movements, with the goal of motivating the reader to go deeper in to the areas that have the greatest potential for missiological applications in his or her own ministry.

The Crusades

From the eleventh to the thirteenth century the Roman church organized about nine military campaigns for liberating the Holy Land (especially Jerusalem and Christ's tomb) from the Muslim occupants. Although some battles were won, the repossessed lands (from a Roman perspective) were eventually lost. The Crusades (*les croisades*) were a major concern of some of the great personalities of the times, such as Saint Louis (*Louis IX*), Urban II, and Bernard of Clairvaux. The Crusades encouraged a mentality that intertwined evangelism, military conquest and the love for adventure. The Crusades in the Holy Land opened the doors for more local crusades in France against both unorthodox groups (the Cathars, also known as Albigensians) and evangelical movements (the Waldenses, *les vaudois*) (Douglas 1978:274).

The Renaissance of the Thirteenth Century

Beginning around 1180, Western Civilization began to experience the greatest period of economic expansion that it had known in a thousand years. Cities started to play an important economic role again, many technological breakthroughs were implemented, and money began to circulate as it had in ancient times. The church flourished during this period, establishing the first universities, building the great gothic cathedrals, and encouraging a renewal of writing. The theological writings of the High Middle Ages were often quite sophisticated, but far from the essential themes of the Gospel (Rivière 1986:50-68).

The Reformation

After two hundred years of economic and demographic setbacks due to the Hundred Years' War and the Black Death, France turned the corner and entered into the Renaissance of the sixteenth century which had recently started in Italy. The first signs of spiritual revival in France came from a group of scholars around the city of Meaux in the early sixteenth century. Under their influence, and that of Martin Luther, John Calvin (*Jean Calvin*) eventually became the chief reformer and spokesman of Protestantism in France and much of Western Europe. At first, the Protestants were tolerated, but by the middle of the sixteenth century persecution became regular (Douglas 1978:830-31).

The Counter Reformation

Because of the turmoil within Christendom caused by the Protestant Reformation, the Roman church, in France and in all of Europe, opened itself up to reform. During the middle of the sixteenth century the Roman church examined and more closely defined the church's doctrines and dogmas such as the Real Presence in the Mass. Worship practices (such as the seven sacraments and the worship of the Virgin and the Saints) were affirmed and defined more precisely. The contents of the Bible were defined to contain the sixty-six traditional books plus the deuterocanonical books; the Vulgate was made the official version of the Bible to be used by

Christians. The celibacy of priests was reaffirmed and better schools were instituted for their training (De Montclos 1988:62-67).

The Catholic reformation was so sweeping and complete that the Roman church kept essentially the same doctrines and practices from the sixteenth century to the middle of the twentieth century. It was Vatican II that would open the doors of change (Douglas 1978:1012-14).

The Wars of Religion and the Edict of Nantes

One of the results of the Counter Reformation was that Protestants were clearly labeled heretics because they rejected so much of Catholic dogma. The Protestants not only angered the Roman church, but also the Kings of France whose royal legitimacy was based on the authority of the church. Various estimates have put the number of Protestant sympathizers between ten and forty percent of the population of France. In 1562, the first group of Protestants was massacred. A civil war began to develop, a war that was not just Papists versus Huguenots, but a war which had many political overtones as several great lords sided with and financed the Protestant movement with the hope of gaining independence from royal authority. The most famous attack against the Protestants was the St. Bartholomew's Day Massacre, August 24, 1572, when the Seine River was said to have turned red from the blood shed by the approximately three thousand Protestants killed, including almost all of the political leaders (Rivière 1986:163-64).

When King Henry III (the leader of the Catholic forces) was assassinated in 1589 by a monk who thought the King was not hard enough on the Protestants, the next in line to become king was Henry of Navarre who was raised as a Protestant by his mother and who was the head of the

Protestant military forces. He seemed to have no real religious convictions, and adopted Catholicism in order to take the throne as Henry IV, who would become the most beloved of all French kings. He is best known for saying "Paris is well worth a Mass" (*"Paris vaut une messe"*) and for his reputation as "The Dirty Old Man" (*Le Vert gallant)*. In 1598, he issued the Edict of Nantes which granted toleration to the Protestants (Rivière 1986:119-20).

However, the Protestants were not tolerated by the following kings, Louis XIII and Louis XIV. Because of the extreme persecution (*les dragonnades*) of the Protestants by Louis XIV, many of them fled to neighboring countries or America, diminishing the small but growing French middle class. Louis XIV revoked the Edict of Nantes in 1685, claiming it was no longer necessary since there were so few Protestants left in his kingdom (Rivière 1986:163-64).

The Enlightenment and the French Revolution

During the Enlightenment (*siècle des lumières*), France was the center of scientific, philosophical, and political analysis and change. All ways of thinking were put into question, especially those concerning religion. For the first time in over a thousand years, one could reject Christianity without losing his or her cultural identity (De Montclos 1988:79-83).

What most marked France during this period was the French Revolution which began in 1789. The Divine Right of the king was no longer recognized; it has been said that when the king was beheaded, God was beheaded as well. As the Revolution grew more and more radical, the Catholic churches were closed down and some were transformed, such as Notre Dame de Paris, into temples for the worship of the Goddess of

120 THE RELIGIOUS HISTORY OF FRANCE

Reason. However, by the end of the century, Catholicism was restored as the official religion of France under Napoleon, and Protestantism (the Reformed Church) was tolerated (Rivière 1986:194-223).

The Nineteenth Century Religious Revivals

The intellectual and social implications of the Enlightenment continued to have a great impact as society grew more and more secular. The Catholic Church became less influential as the State took primary responsibility for the education of children. The Reformed Church began to suffer the consequences of liberalism and lost much of its evangelical fervor. Secular quasi-religious organizations such as the Freemasons (*les francs-maçons*) filled part of the sociological void (De Montclos 1988:90-95).

As in times of past turmoil, the Catholic Church turned to Rome for stability. In 1848 the Pope defined the dogma of the Immaculate Conception (*la conception immaculée*) reviving much enthusiasm for Mariolatrous Catholicism. The idea of an independent French Catholic Church (Gallicanism) was put to rest at Vatican I (1869-1870) when the idea of papal infallibility was accepted as dogma. Many practicing Catholics in France actively promoted a return to a conservative Catholicism and one concrete result of this fervor was the construction of the Sacré-Coeur Basilica in Paris (De Montclos 1988:95-101).

In the Reformed churches, many pastors began to see that Protestantism was losing its evangelical fervor because of the influence of rationalism and materialism. Beginning in French-speaking Switzerland, and then moving to France, *le Réveil* (The Awakening) was led by pastors who began to emphasize once again the authority of the Bible and the need for personal conversion. Some pastors within this evangelical current decided to stay within the Reformed church, others decided that a radical break was needed. Several Reformed churches broke away from the denomination and became independent. Other churches during these periods of revival saw individuals leave the Reformed churches and start new evangelical churches, especially Brethren churches. Baptists and Methodists from England came as missionaries and started several evangelical churches as well, often profiting from the revivals in the other churches (De Montclos 1986:106-108).

The Anglo-Saxon Missionary Influx after World War II

Although some Protestant evangelical missionaries, mainly from England, had come to France before World War II, it was especially after the War that large numbers of missionaries, principally Americans, came to France to start new churches. Many soldiers who had fought to liberate the Continent from Nazism were surprised at the spiritual wasteland that they found here and later came back as missionaries. Other Europeans as well, from the traditionally Protestant countries, also began evangelistic efforts in France. New churches were planted and the people who these new churches attracted were often from traditionally Protestant families or immigrants from Africa and the Caribbean (*les Antilles*), as well as some who had either a non-religious or Catholic background (Dagon 1993:39).

In the last quarter of the twentieth century, as the Roman Catholic and Reformed churches were quickly losing members, the young evangelical churches continued to grow. Many of the conservative, non-charismatic evangelical churches formed and joined the *Fédération Evangélique de France*. Most of the Pentecostal churches identified themselves with the Assemblies of God (*les Assemblées de Dieu*) while the *Fédération Protestante de France* included a great variety of Protestant churches: both evangelical and non-evangelical Reformed churches, Lutheran churches having their origin in the German speaking part of France, churches open to the charismatic movement, and churches started by Southern Baptist missionaries (Fédération Evangélique de France 2000:488-494). In 2010, after many years of discussion, the evangelical churches from these diverse backgrounds worked together to form the *Conseil National des Evangéliques de France* (The National Council of Evangelicals of France) to better represent the interests of French evangelicals.

The Third Millennium

It is impossible to predict the future. However, there are several trends that look like they will have a great influence on what will become the religious history of France for the third millennium.

1. Greater Government Control: With a greater diffusion of information due to the progress made during the Age of Communication, more and more esoteric and cult-like religions and philosophies are available to the French. Already the government has tried to limit the establishment of new religions in order to protect society. This trend is likely to continue and increase, meaning that, because of mistrust, young evangelical churches will be scrutinized more and more closely. In light of this trend, missionaries must be all the more careful to be beyond reproach and must do all they can to identify themselves with the evangelical movements

that already have a strong French identity. Young churches must be established in ways that meet government regulations (especially concerning transparency in finances) and do all that they can to not come across as foreign cults.

2. Changes in the Catholic Church: Since Vatican II, the Catholic Church has become somewhat more open to other Christian religions and less dogmatic concerning their own doctrines. It is also quickly losing members; less than sixty percent of the French are baptized. Since these two trends are likely to continue, it is possible that there might greater cooperation between evangelical Protestants and Catholics in, for example, evangelism projects and the sharing of facilities. If this would lead to a greater number of people coming to Christ, the missionary must be open to considering the possibilities that might be available.

3. A Greater Muslim Influence: Approximately fifteen percent of French youth now consider themselves Muslim, primarily those of Arab descent. Islam is the second most populous religion in France and in many senses the most visible. A typical French youth will know more about Ramadan than about lent. If one were to mention God's will, a person might think of Jihad before he or she thinks of the teachings of Jesus. Since the time of Charles Martel, Muslims have been considered the enemies of France, so practicing Muslims are looked down upon by much of the French population. The net effect of all this is that the popular view of God is being less defined by traditional Catholic dogma and more so by Islam. For

missionaries, this means that they will need to make sure that the Gospel message they present clearly includes biblical teaching about the nature of God. It cannot be assumed that those who believe in God will have any idea of the Trinity, God's moral nature, or any idea of how he has worked previously in human history. Some missionaries have specifically targeted practicing Muslims, but others have found that it is more effective to reach Muslims by targeting neighborhoods that have a high Arab population.

4. Fewer Missionaries: A final trend that might be seen in the twenty-first century is the presence of fewer Anglo-Saxon missionaries. Since in many evangelical circles it is not "politically correct" to say that most Catholics are not Christians in the New Testament sense of the term, it is becoming more and more difficult to recruit new missionaries to come to France. Likewise, many consider France to be evangelized because the Bible is available in French, even though the vast majority of the population has never heard a comprehensible presentation of the Gospel. This means that the missionaries who do come to work in France will have an even greater responsibility to clearly present the Gospel, establish Bible believing churches, and train the leaders whom God raises up to reach the rest of the country for Christ. Throughout the history of France, God has been at work in the lives of various individuals and communities. In His name, both great and horrible things have been accomplished. May all those who read this book find the exact role that God would have them play in the continuing story of France's religious history.

The Church in the 2nd and 3rd Millenniums 125

REFERENCES CITED

Benedict of Nursia
    c. 540 *The Holy Rule of St. Benedict.* 1949 Edition. Trans. By Verheyen, Boniface. Atchison, Kansas: St. Benedict's Abbey. www.kansasmonks.org/ruleofstbenedict.html

Burnand, Yves
    1996 *Les Gallo-Romains.* Collection *Que sais-je ?* Paris : Presses Universitaires de France.

Cassian, John
    c. 435 *The Conferences.* Edgar C. S Gibson, trans. In *The Nicene and Post-Nicene Fathers.* Second Series, Volume XI. Schaff, Philip, and Wace, Henry, eds. Edinburgh: T & T Clark.

Césaire of Arles, et al.
529 *The Canons of the Council of Orange.* http://www.reformed.org/documents/canons_of_orange.html

Dagon, Gérard
1993 *Panorama de la France Evangélique.* Vol. 1. Yerres, France : Editions Barnabas.

De Montclos, Xavier
1988 *Histoire Religieuse de la France.* Collection *Que sais-je ?* Paris : Presses Univesitaires de France.

Douglas, J.D., ed.
1978 *The New International Dictionary of the Christian Church.* Revised Edition. Grand Rapids, MI: Zondervan.

Einhard
c. 833 "The Life of Charlemagne." In *Two Lives of Charlemagne.* Lewis Thorpe, trans. London: Penguin Books.

Eusebius
324 *The History of the Church.* G.A. Williamson, trans. Andrew Louth, ed. London : Penguin Books.

Fédération Evangélique de France
2000 *Annuaire Evangélique 2000/2001.* Dozulé, France : Editions Barnabas.

Frémy, Dominique and Frémy, Michelle
    1998   *Quid*. 1999 edition. Paris: Editions Robert Laffont.

Gregory of Tours
    591   *The History of the Franks*. Lewis Thorpe, trans. London: Penguin Books.

Goscinny
    1975   *La Grande Traversée*. Paris : Dargaud Editeur.

Latourette, Kenneth Scott
    1975   *A History of Christianity: Volume 1: to A.D. 1500*. Revised Edition. San Francisco, CA: HarperCollins.

Neill, Stephen
    1986   *A History of Christian Missions*. Revised Edition. Chadwick Owen, ed. London: Penguin Books.

Rey, Alain, ed.
    1987   *Le Petit Robert 2*. Revised Edition. Paris : Le Robert.

Rivière, Daniel
    1986   *Histoire de la France*. Paris : Hachette.

Salter, Louis
    1909 *False Decretals.* In *The Catholic Encyclopedia*, Vol. 5. Robert Appleton Company. www.newadvent.org/cathen/05773a.htm

Severus, Sulpicius
    c. 395 *Life of Martin of Tours.* In *Early Christian Lives.* Caroline White, ed. And trans. New York: Penguin Books, 1998.

Vincent de Lérins
    c. 435 *The Commonitory.* C. A. Heurtley, trans. In *The Nicene and Post-Nicene Fathers.* Second Series, Volume XI. Philip Schaff, and Henry Wace, eds. Edinburgh: T & T Clark.

Index

A

Abbé Pierre, 85
abbess, 65
abbeys, 80, 96, 97, 103
abbot, 77, 79, 80, 81
abbots, 79, 102, 106
Africa, 93, 121
Against Heresies, 24
agape, 53
Aix-la-Chapelle, 97, 99
Alamanni, 60, 62
Alans, 59
Albigensians, 116
Alcibiades, 24
Alcuin, 99, 100
All Saints Day, 13
alternative medicine, 11
Americanization, 15
Amiens, 38
anchoritic, 37
Apollo, 9
Aquitaine, 44, 57, 106
Arabs, 103, 123, 124
archbishops, 45, 97
Arians, 45, 57, 58, 63, 70, 71
aristocracy, 36
Arius, 46, 71
Arles, 25, 34, 45, 69, 71, 72, 128
Arnulf, 92, 93
Ascension, 69
asceticism, 83
Asia, 6, 20
aspersion, 7
Assemblies of God, 122
Astérix, 5, 10, 15
astrology, 13
atheism, 23
Attila the Hun, 59
Augustine, 40

Autun, 59
Auxerre, 59

B

Baal, 9
baptism, 2, 34, 38, 42, 45, 53, 61, 62, 72, 74, 75, 88, 100, 101, 123
baptismal regeneration, 45, 88
Baptists, 52, 121, 122
barbarians, 35, 42, 43, 44, 45, 56, 58, 59, 60, 75, 84
Belgium, 6, 102
Benedict, 40, 76, 77, 80, 127
Benedictine Rule, 40, 76, 77, 80, 101
Bernard, 38, 116
Bethlehem, 40
Béziers, 44, 45
Bible, 4, 12, 14, 16, 17, 18, 24, 28, 29, 40, 42, 45, 46, 47, 48, 49, 52, 53, 90, 99, 108, 117, 120, 123, 124
birth control, 89, 90
bishops, 20, 24, 25, 34, 36, 38, 40, 41, 45, 48, 58, 59, 60, 62, 63, 64, 65, 66, 67, 68, 69, 71, 73, 75, 76, 77, 81, 82, 84, 96, 97, 103, 104, 105, 106
Black Death, 117
Blandina, 20, 21, 22, 30
Boniface, 72, 94, 95, 127
Boniface II, 72
Bourges, 26
Brethren, 121
Brittany, 7, 8, 18, 57
Buddhism, 51
Burgundians, 57, 63, 70
Burgundy, 61, 70
Bussy-St.-Georges, 85

Byzantine Empire, 94

C

Calvin, John, 117
Cannes, 45
Capétiens, 103
Caribbean, 121
Carolingians, v, 91, 92, 99, 100, 101, 102, 103, 107
Cassian, John, 40, 41, 71, 76, 127
Cassiodorus, 78
catechism, 41, 85
catechumens, 42, 45
Cathars, 116
Catholic, 2, 13, 16, 30, 46, 47, 51, 53, 55, 56, 59, 63, 67, 70, 85, 88, 89, 90, 100, 105, 111, 118, 119, 120, 121, 123, 124, 130
celibacy, 74, 81, 89, 118
Celts, 6, 7, 10, 12, 13
cenobitic, 37, 40
ceremonies, 7, 9, 16, 26, 41, 43, 44, 69, 70, 101
Césaire, 69, 71, 72, 128
Cesar, 8
Charlemagne, 76, 92, 96, 97, 98, 99, 100, 101, 102, 103, 107, 108, 128
Charles Martel, 93, 94, 123
Charles the Bald, 102, 103
Charles the Simple, 104
Childeric I, 59
Chlodovald, 66
Christendom, 94, 95, 117
Christianization, 35, 41, 72
Christmas, 62, 98
Chrysostom, John, 40
church planting, 13, 26, 28, 30, 31, 108, 109
Clair, 44
Clairvaux, 116
Clement, 35, 105
Clementine I, 41

Clermont-Ferrand, 25, 68, 82
Clotilda, 61, 62, 65, 83
Clovis, 56, 57, 59, 60, 61, 62, 63, 64, 65, 66, 70, 83
Cluny, 106, 111
Columban, 76, 77
Columbanus, 76
Compiègne, 64
Conseil National des Evangéliques de France, 122
Constance Chlore, 27
Constantine, 27, 34, 35, 47, 105
Constantinople, 40, 56
Constantius, 45
convents, 78
Council of Orange, 71, 72, 74, 88, 101, 128
Council of Trent, 47
Counter Reformation, 105, 117, 118
Crusades, 116
Cuise, 64
Cybele, 9

D

Dagobert, 25
Decretals of Pseudo-Isadore, 104
Denmark, 103
Diocletian, 26
Dionysius, 25, 30
discipline, 79, 80, 81
Divine Right, 119
Donatist controversy, 34
Donatus, 46
druid, 7, 18
Druid, 5
druidism, 8, 13, 14, 18
druids, 7, 8, 13

E

Easter, 25, 76
Edict of Nantes, 118, 119

Eldest Daughter of the Church, 1, 62
emperor, 23, 27, 34, 35, 36, 38, 56, 94, 98, 101, 102
emperors, 7, 35, 92
England, 1, 73, 94, 95, 108, 121
Enlightenment, 119, 120
episcopate, 38
esoterica, 13
Eunomius, 46
European Community, 92, 108
Eusebius, 20, 23, 24, 25, 73, 128
evangelism, 4, 12, 25, 26, 31, 37, 41, 42, 44, 50, 51, 69, 76, 77, 85, 95, 100, 101, 111, 112, 113, 114, 116, 121, 123
evangelization, 37-38, 42-43, 70, 95
ex voto, 9, 16, 17

F

faith, 11, 16, 21, 23, 24, 30, 36, 41, 45, 46, 48, 51, 53, 55, 61, 70, 72, 73, 100, 101
False Decretals, 104, 130
Faustus of Riez, 71
Fédération Evangélique de France, 121, 128
Fédération Protestante de France, 122
feudal lords, 104, 106
feudal system, 96, 97, 109
feuding lords, 104
Fleury, 77
Franciade, 26
Franklin, Benjamin, 29
Franks, 13, 55, 56, 57, 59, 60, 61, 62, 63, 64, 65, 68, 70, 73, 75, 76, 92, 93, 94, 95, 96, 97, 129
free will, 40, 72
Freemasons, 120
French Revolution, 26, 61, 119
Friesland, 95

G

Galatians, 6
Gallic independence, 15, 40
Gallicanism, 120
Gaul, 5, 7, 8, 9, 10, 12, 14, 15, 16, 18, 19, 20, 23, 25, 27, 29, 30, 33, 34, 35, 36, 37, 38, 40, 41, 44, 45, 56, 57, 58, 60, 63, 68, 70, 71, 72, 73, 75, 76, 77, 78, 86, 89, 92, 101
Gauls, 5, 6, 7, 9, 10, 12, 18, 19, 34, 58, 63
Geneviève, 59
Germanus, 59
Germany, 6, 60, 73, 95, 102, 108
globalization, 13
Goar, 59
Gospel, vii, 3, 4, 11, 15, 16, 18, 19, 24, 25, 29, 33, 36, 41, 44, 47, 48, 49, 50, 62, 69, 83, 85, 95, 111, 112, 113, 117, 123, 124
Goths, 57, 63, 65, 70
grace, 40, 72, 87, 101, 114
Great Britain, 6, 59
Greek, 6, 9, 24, 25, 35, 67, 68, 76
Greeks, 6
Gregory of Tours, 25, 26
Gregory the Great, 25, 26, 55, 60, 61, 62, 63, 64, 65, 66, 67, 68, 70, 71, 72, 73, 77, 79, 81, 82, 89, 94, 104, 106, 129
Guntram, 65
gypsies, 13

H

Halloween, 13
Hamilton, Alexander, 29
healing, 7, 9, 10, 11
Hélène, 27
Henry III, 118
Henry IV, 119

Henry of Navarre, 118
Hercules, 9
hermits, 40, 75
Hildebrand, 106
Hillary of Poitiers, 38, 45
Hitler, 92
Hugh Capet, 102
Huguenots, 118
Hungary, 37, 103
Huns, 58

I

icons, 94
immersion, 7
immigrants, 28, 86, 121
intellectuals, 49
Iran, 59
Ireland, 6, 75, 76, 95, 108
Irenaeus, 20, 24, 25, 27, 28
Iron Age, 6
Islam, 93, 123
Italy, 6, 44, 57, 59, 73, 76, 78, 95, 102, 117

J

Jefferson, Thomas, 29
Jesus, 10, 18, 28, 30, 37, 39, 49, 50, 53, 123
Jesus Christ, 11, 15, 16, 18, 21, 22, 23, 25, 27, 30, 34, 36, 37, 38, 39, 41, 45, 48, 49, 50, 52, 53, 55, 62, 66, 70, 72, 74, 75, 76, 79, 80, 81, 83, 90, 101, 110, 112, 113, 116, 123
Jihad, 123
Julian the Apostate, 34
Julius Cesar, 6, 18
Jupiter, 9

L

Lascaux, 5
Latin, 7, 9, 20, 24, 75, 95, 98
Lérins, 45, 71
lèse-majesté, 23
Lewis the Pious, 102
Licinius, 34
Ligué, 38
Limoges, 25
literary analysis, 53
liturgy, 98
Lombard, 94
Lothar I, 64, 65
Louis V, 103
Louis XIII, 119
Louis XIV, 92, 119
Lutherans, 122
Luxembourg, 102
Luxeuil, 76
Lyons, 20, 23, 37, 106

M

Maas River, 95
Macedonius, 46
Mars, 9
Marseilles, 40, 41
Martin of Tours, 37, 38, 39, 40, 41, 42, 44, 45, 103, 117, 130
martyrs, 20, 23, 25, 27, 30, 37, 43, 44, 100
masses, 8, 16, 35, 36, 37, 43, 44, 47, 51, 52, 59, 69, 72, 74, 88, 106, 109, 113
May, 69
mayor, 14, 109
Mayor of the Palace, 92, 93, 94, 95
Meaux, 117
Mercury, 9, 12
Merovech, 66
Mérovée, 55
Merovingians, v, 55, 62, 63, 64, 65, 66, 67, 70, 71, 73, 74, 78, 83,

91, 92, 93, 94, 96
Methodists, 121
Milan, 34, 45
Minerva, 9
missionaries, 2, 3, 4, 10-20, 25-31, 37, 47-55, 67, 75, 83, 85, 86, 87, 88, 90, 94-95, 100, 107-115, 121-124
Mithra, 9
monasteries, 38, 39, 40, 44, 45, 59, 65, 66, 67, 70, 71, 74, 75, 76, 77, 78, 79, 80, 81, 82, 99, 101, 106, 111
monasticism, 37, 40, 74, 75, 78
monk, 37, 40, 81, 83, 106
monks, 37-40, 45, 70, 75-83, 89, 99, 100, 106
Monte Cassino, 76, 77
Montmartre, 25
mountains, 6, 8, 10, 12
Muslims, 74, 93, 94, 116, 123

N

Napoleon, 92, 120
Narbonne, 25
Nazi, 28
Netherlands, 95, 102
New Age, 13, 51
Nicean, 57, 58, 67
Nicholas I, 105
nicolaïsme, 104
niveau culturel, 86, 87
Normandy, 104
North Africa, 34
North America, 2, 15, 17, 29, 31, 85, 87, 112, 119
North Americans, 2, 4, 10, 14, 15, 17, 28, 29-31, 39, 52, 55, 85, 91, 107, 108, 110-112, 115
Notre Dame, 119
Novatian, 46
nuns, 39, 89

O

obedience, 77, 80, 81, 95
Obélix, 5, 10
oblations, 9
offerings, 6
Origen, 35
orthodox, 45, 47, 52, 61, 85
orthodoxy, 45, 46, 53, 59
Ostrogoths, 57

P

pagan, 34, 35, 41, 42, 43, 57, 59, 60, 61, 67, 68, 69, 75, 95, 100
paganism, 10, 13, 35, 70
Paine, Thomas, 29
Panoramix, 5
pantheon, 8, 9, 18
papal supremacy, 105
Papists, 118
Paris, 12, 13, 25, 27, 51, 56, 59, 66, 94, 102, 119, 120
parishes, 96
Parisians, 51
Pastoral Rule, 73
Paul, 73, 82, 113
Pelagianism, 59
Pentecostals, 121
Pepin, 93, 94, 95, 96
persecution, 19, 20, 23, 24, 25, 26, 27, 35, 37, 48, 64, 117, 119
Poitiers, 38, 45, 93
polygamy, 76
Ponticus, 22
popes, 30, 40, 41, 59, 72, 77, 80, 89, 94, 95, 96, 98, 101, 105, 106, 120
Pothinus, 20, 23, 24, 30
prayer, 9, 11, 39, 40, 79, 82
preaching, 41, 67, 69-70
predestination, 41, 47, 72, 88
priests, 7, 41, 64, 69, 74, 78, 89, 97,

98, 104, 118
Primulac, 44
purgatory, 74, 88

R

Real Presence, 117
Reformation, 48, 105, 117, 118
Reformed churches, 52, 120, 121, 122
Reims, 62
relics, 38, 43, 44, 52, 69, 73, 77, 104
Rémi, 62
Renaissance, 99, 116, 117
Rhone Valley, 20, 24
rock formations, 6, 12
Rogations, 69
Rollo, 104
Roman Empire, 7, 8, 19, 35, 36, 56, 94, 95, 97, 98, 100, 108
Romans, 5, 6, 8, 9, 15, 18, 35, 56, 86
Rome, 2, 5, 6, 7, 8, 9, 10, 12, 13, 14, 15, 18, 19, 20, 24, 25, 26, 29, 33, 34, 35, 36, 37, 40, 41, 44, 46, 47, 50, 52, 56, 57, 58, 59, 60, 61, 62, 63, 67, 68, 72, 73, 75, 76, 78, 88, 90, 91, 93, 94, 95, 96, 97, 98, 100, 104, 105, 106, 108, 116, 117, 118, 120, 121

S

Sabellius, 46
sacraments, 96, 104, 117
Sacré-Coeur Basilica, 120
sacrifice, 8, 16, 23
sacrifices, 7, 9, 23, 30
Saint Bartholomew's Day Massacre, 118
Saint Louis, 116
Saint-Benoît-sur-Loire, 77

saints, 24, 43, 44, 52, 74
Saracens, 103
Saturnius, 25, 30
Scandinavians, 103
Scriptures, 46, 76
Seine River, 104, 118
semi-Pelagianism, 41, 47, 71
Septuagint, 25
Severus, 38, 39, 40, 42, 44, 45, 130
sexuality, 89, 90
Shepherd of Hermas, 25
shrines, 41, 43
simony, 104
Soissons, 56, 60
sorcery, 18
Spain, 57, 63, 65, 73, 93
springs, 6, 8, 9, 10, 11
St. Denis, 25, 26, 94
statues, 7, 9, 57, 69
suburbs, 28, 87
Sulpicius Severus, 37, 44
Sunday School, 28
superstitions, 10, 18, 26
Switzerland, 6, 57, 102, 120
syncretism, 12, 15

T

teens, 48, 53
territorial spirits, 12
thanksgiving, 9, 16, 17
Theodosius, 35
Theudebert, 66
Thierry III, 93
tithe, 96, 98
Toulouse, 25
Tours, 25, 26, 37, 38, 44, 45, 55, 60, 61, 62, 63, 64, 65, 66, 67, 68, 70, 79, 81, 82, 129, 130
tradition, 24, 28, 47, 64, 68
Tradition, 46, 61
Trinitarian, 45
Trinity, 70, 71, 123

U

urban exodus, 42, 51, 67, 68
Urban II, 116
Ursinus, 26

V

Vandals, 58
Vatican I, 120
Vatican II, 118, 123
Vercingétorix, 7, 15, 38
Vettius Epagathus, 20
vicar, 73
Victor, 24
Vienne, 20, 23, 37, 69
Vikings, 103, 104
villas, 43, 51
Vincent de Lérins, 45, 46, 53, 71, 130

Visigoths, 57
visual aids, 52
Vosges Mountains, 76
Vulcan, 9
Vulgate, 117

W

Waldenses, 116
Washington, George, 29
William the Pious, 106
Willibrord, 95
Winfrith, 95
witch doctors, 13
witchcraft, 13, 18
World War II, 17, 121
worship, 8, 9, 12, 16, 20, 29, 36, 43, 44, 49, 53, 57, 62, 94, 117, 119

138

www.ingramcontent.com/pod-product-compliance
Lightning Source LLC
Chambersburg PA
CBHW071510040426
42444CB00008B/1583